Dear Reader:

I am so glad that CT Shackleford wrote *Can We Talk?: Claiming the Happiness You Deserve*. Why? Because the things that she says within the pages needed to be said. Women have to realize that despite what society has attempted to drill into our heads over and over again, we are the most valuable things in existence. Yet, we are still undervalued, underappreciated and misunderstood. For the past 14 years, I have been leading a revolution for female empowerment. *Can We Talk?* is a great milestone in that revolution. Hopefully, you will take all of the information contained within and apply it to your life.

The only limitations in life exist in our minds. You can be whatever you want to be. You can experience whatever you want to experience. You can be as happy and content as you want to be. You must speak all of that into existence and stop lowering your standards to meet your lifestyle but adjust your lifestyle to meet your standards. Never settle for less than what you desire, or deserve. Embrace it! Claim it! Speak it into existence! Most importantly, never, ever give up. Every day is a gift and with the right attitude, all the cards will fall perfectly into place; especially when it comes to love. Do not seek love; attract it. By changing your focus, your beliefs, and transforming your weaknesses into your strengths, you will get everything that you feel that you deserve and more.

As always, thanks for the support shown to the Strebor Books International family. We appreciate the love. For more information on our titles, please visit www.zanestore.com and you can find me on my personal website: www.eroticanoir.com. You can also join my online social network at www.planetzane.org.

Blessings,

Zane

Zane
Publisher
Strebor Books International
www.simonandschuster.com/streborbooks

ZANE PRESENTS

Can We Talk?

Claiming the Happiness You Deserve

ZANE PRESENTS

Can We Talk?

Claiming the Happiness You Deserve

CT Shackleford

SBI

STREBOR BOOKS

NEW YORK LONDON TORONTO SYDNEY

Strebor Books
P.O. Box 6505
Largo, MD 20792
http://www.streborbooks.com

This book is a work of nonfiction.

© 2011 by CT Shackleford

ISBN 978-1-59309-383-9
ISBN 978-1-4516-4707-5 (e-book)
LCCN 2011928051

First Strebor Books trade paperback edition October 2011

Cover design: www.mariondesigns.com
Cover photograph: © Keith Saunders/Marion Designs

1 0 9 8 7 6 5 4 3 2 1

Manufactured in the United States of America

For information regarding special discounts for bulk purchases,
please contact Simon & Schuster Special Sales at 1-866-506-1949
or business@simonandschuster.com

The Simon & Schuster Speakers Bureau can bring authors to your live event.
For more information or to book an event, contact the Simon & Schuster Speakers
Bureau at 1-866-248-3049 or visit our website at www.simonspeakers.com.

This book is dedicated to those who dare to be happy
and those who struggle to be.

Acknowledgments

Thank you, God. Without you, *nothing* is possible.

To my mama, Annie Mae. Without your teachings, I would have struggled harder to be the woman that I have become. You are an avid reader and because of your passion, you were able to affectionately share with me my need to improve my work.

To my husband, Namon. Thank you for being the man you are. Had you been a different man, I could have become a different woman. Marriage has a way of changing people, and sometimes not for the better. I am both grateful and proud, that I married a man whose intention has only been to love me the best way he knows how. Another thanks to you, my *"Lover Man,"* because you supported me in writing this book, even when you weren't painted in the best light and you learned things about the life I had before you. You took it the way a real man would—with courage, acceptance, and understanding. You have been my greatest supporter and I love you most because you have *always* had my back.

To my children, Kyle and Trey, I love you both more than "this much!" The two of you are an ever-constant reminder of what is possible. You are my inspiration to want more and do better.

To my sisters, Valerie Tyes (my personal Sous Chef) and Sylvia Cook. Valerie, thank you for your *constant* support. My endless appreciation goes in no lesser measure to my extended family and friends that supported me, the way they each could, in this endeavor.

Their encouragement was exactly what I needed to complete this work. Dana Hampton, Sallie Sistrunk, Danielle Withers, Valencia Robinson, Mishari Hanible, Dexter Reid, Angela Tartt, Courtney Cook, John T. Cook, JR, Nicole Tyes (Glamour), Pearlie Harris, Gregory & Makini Coleman, Robert Gordon, Trista Blake, Bonita Hampton, Amber Banks, Sharon Banks, Natalie G. Owens, Laura Hall, Demetrice Coleman, Verna Love, Andrea Thompson, Tanya Smallwood, Lori Walker, and Chatelle Hawthorne.

To Zane and Charmaine Parker... Where do I start? I have no words to express the gratitude I have for this publishing opportunity. Thank you doesn't seem enough, so I will say, "Thank you, thank you and thank you to infinity!" Also, I want to thank everyone at Strebor Books/Simon & Schuster that had, in any way, anything to do with seeing my dream realized.

Lastly, I want to thank all of the people that provided the experiences necessary in order to make this book a possibility. I am grateful for the experiences of my past—the good, the bad, and especially the ugly. Had I not had them, I wouldn't have been able to appreciate the wonderful life I have been blessed to live. The person we grow to become is a combination of our home life and our "street" life. The manner in which we bring the two experiences together determines how we plot our course through life. With this considered, I think my mother and I did an exceptional job of raising me. Because I am, *truly* and *humbly*, the woman I want to be!

Prologue

There are so many things that I don't understand. One of them is why we women act surprised when we've been done wrong by a man, for the one-thousandth time. Ladies, it is because **WE** have allowed it! Women have taken on many roles over the past few decades. Roles that include being a mother, career woman, and all around caretaker. However, a man's role has not fully evolved as a woman's. Decades ago, even if a man was not involved in the rearing of his children, he was *at least* the breadwinner.

Today, women are bringing home the bacon and frying it up in the pan. And at the same time, we are also changing diapers, cooking and cleaning, while the man's role has essentially remained unchanged, so to speak. Therefore, it is in that same spirit that I suggest that many men are nothing more than boys dressed in men's clothing. They don't have to do anything but be themselves, while we bend ourselves over backward to accommodate them (their needs and desires).

Another thing I don't understand is why we women blame anything and everything for not having the life we want. If you think the life that you want is about your having the perfect man and producing perfect children, while having the perfect job, let me put a stop to your illusions now. None of it is possible, except maybe the perfect job because of its requirements—having the right connections and/or educational foundation. However, the perfect job does have a common thread with what women may consider to be the perfect man and perfect children. They all have personal involvement and accountability for their outcome.

There is no such thing as perfection when it comes to the relationships that exist between people; especially the relationship between a woman and man. It is possible, however, to have a good and decent relationship with the man in your life, once you first have that relationship with yourself. It is also possible to have well-behaved and smart children when you learn that having them is much more than a notion.

When children are born into the world, they need more from us than food, clothing and shelter. They desperately need and deserve to have our attention, unconditional love and, above all else, to be disciplined. As mothers, we can't give it to them until we are in the position to do so. Children who don't get what they need growing up become adults who require more of the same—attention, unconditional love, and discipline! We have to pay attention to ourselves in order to give ourselves what we need from ourselves. We have to love ourselves despite our own imperfections, and be grateful for the body and the life that we have. If it is recognized that we don't have what we want or desire, we have to have the discipline to change our lives.

All relationships, especially those of the married kind, are not for the weak, immature, insecure or selfish. No one is perfect. But at some point in time, in our lives we will exhibit one or more of these traits. Nonetheless, it is not having these traits that is important, but how they manifest themselves or the intention in which they are used.

If I may be so bold, I'd like to share that my husband once told me that I *saved* his life! I am humbled that he thinks that I deserve the credit. But let me just say, I did not change him. I influenced the change he made in himself by not making excuses for his behavior and holding him accountable for his side of the bargain in this relationship. That's important for me to say, seeing as though I am not his mother, nor do I want to be.

When I married him, I was determined to have a grown-up relationship with him, whether he wanted it or not! It is no laughing matter to me when I hear the common comment being made by many women, such as: "I have three children"—meaning two children and a husband! I can't lie and say that my husband doesn't sometimes act "child-like," but so can I when I want *my way*!

Once we said "I DO," the suave, independent, intelligent, chivalrous man somewhat disappeared. Because when we dated, he was on his "best" behavior. That said, in the present, my husband, for the most part, is a full-grown man in the ways that are most important to me. I can depend on him for whatever my needs may be. If I am hungry, he feeds me. If I am tired, weary, or feeling a little disconnected, he allows me time to be alone. He honors me by being the kind of husband that I can trust with my person. But trust me, it has not always been this way. Sometimes we both backslide—even he is fully willing to admit this. His willingness to do so is the very thing that makes him a man in my eyes!

I am somewhat frustrated by the wealth of self-help information out there; especially the material formulated for women. Like how to find the man of your dreams or the guide to understanding your man, etc. Information that has more to do with who is wrong in the relationship instead of trying to get *it* right, for the relationship's sake.

I started writing this book because of my desire to get people, especially women, talking more about what is necessary for personal happiness and longevity in a healthy relationship. Let me qualify it because someone asked me a while back, "What makes you qualified to write a book like this?" I will start off by telling you what I am not—a feminist, psychologist or expert. But what I am is a woman who, on a daily basis, has experienced people, women especially, drowning in their own existence; seemingly unable to make a difference in their lives, or in the lives of the many people who depend on them for their survival. I know this to be true because of my own experiences. So in short, it has been my experiences that have made me qualified to write what I have written on these pages. Because living is learning!

My hope for this book is that it will spark dialogue between the sexes about why we women continue to ask others what they need from us to make them happy! Why does the existence of our life and the happiness we experience in it have to revolve around others; especially around the men in our lives? What he wants in us, what makes *him* happy, and how *he* ticks! Rather, I believe that we need to be talking about what we expect and want for ourselves and from ourselves, what makes us happy, what we need and expect from others, and what makes *us* tick!

Where did that concept of asking others what they want from us come from and why does it continue to exist today, in the year 2011? Why does the information out there continue to be about us asking the world of people, especially men, about what they want in us, rather than what we want from ourselves, from a man, from a relationship, and from life. This book will attempt to answer all these questions and, yes, even provide solutions. I guarantee it—if we are willing to be as invested in ourselves as we are in what makes others happy, we will have the life that we want and deserve.

Genesis

Where Does It Begin?

The Chosen Sex

1

Why are men the chosen sex? Why do we give up so much of ourselves, including the act of being ourselves, just so they can be comfortable with their choices, in their world and in their own skin?

From the time they are born, they are treated differently, royally. My first-born child is a girl and when she was an infant, she received a lot of attention from people. But my second child is a boy, and let me just say, the attention he receives is astounding. Granted, he was a beautiful baby, but no more beautiful than she was at that age. I even had someone comment to me (as I was holding my infant baby girl), "I just love baby boys," while looking at my beautiful baby girl. I couldn't figure out if that was an insult directed toward me for having had a girl, or to my baby girl for having being born female.

When I was pregnant with my second baby and being unaware of the gender (as with my first pregnancy), I said to a close friend, "I'll be glad when this is over," meaning the pregnancy because I had no intention of having any more! She replied, "What if it's a girl?" And I replied, "What *if* it's a girl? We'll just have two girls!" She seemed as though she couldn't believe what she was hearing. As if she assumed we would try and try and try until we succeeded in having a male child. I know of a few instances where women have tried, sometimes unsuccessfully, to have a male child, producing many girls, trying to have that boy because the man in her life wants a junior. I don't understand it; unless their pockets were full or there was a desire for a large family, I can't tell what the hell they were thinking.

One day, my daughter and I went to a prior place of my employment where I ran into a co-worker. She looked over in our general direction. She walked over and said hello and asked me, "Where's your boy?" I was baffled, because she didn't acknowledge my daughter's presence. I told her that he was at home with daddy and she shrugged her shoulders as if to say, "Oh, well," and went on with the rest of her day, still without acknowledging my daughter's presence.

We teach our boys that all they have to do is be themselves, and the world of women will flock to them and bend to their every desire. On some level, I was once one of those women. I can remember the first time it was indicated to me that I was to be flexible to a man's will. It was just after my grandfather passed away; I was about twenty years old. The time immediately after a death is when people are constantly around; bringing food, eating and drinking. The music was playing (that was nothing new in our household). A male family acquaintance was there and he wanted to dance with me this one particular evening. He was a little tipsy and I explained the situation to a female relative of mine. I was expecting some assistance from her to help me out of it, but what I got was her saying: "Aw, just dance with the boy. He ain't gonna hurt you; he's just drunk." I was a little taken aback at her response. There was no consideration for my feelings; it was only about what *he* wanted, and he was **nobody**!

By *nobody*, I mean he was simply someone we knew, and not that well; he was no one that we depended on for anything. Well, I didn't want to dance with him, and I didn't. I wanted to respect my own feelings, rather than his. Who the hell was he that I would give up who or what I was to be pleasing to him? Yuck! And who was she to think that it was okay to tell a twenty-year-old to do something, or be something, that someone else wanted her to be?

Aside from men being the chosen sex, there is also a double standard that exists between the sexes. I had a former male co-worker comment to me that he didn't think that men are the chosen sex. He said, "I don't think we are the chosen ones. I think we are cursed. Our battles are rarely understood and appreciated. I think that one of the biggest hurdles in relationships is the lack of understanding between a man and a woman." I agreed with his observation. And I offered him this explanation: "I agree that there is definitely a misunderstanding between men and women. But I still believe that men are the chosen sex." As you continue to read on, hopefully you will begin to see where I am coming from.

However, I feel that it is the disparity with double standards that has caused many of the misunderstandings. Moreover, how can relationships change for the better if the sexes are not willing to see their part in not merely the success of, but also the failure of their relationships? I believe when it comes to those double standards, some are necessary. Just like in the movies, the actor has his or her role to play. Double standards are necessary; they determine the part we play in real life. I feel that a woman should carry herself a certain way and I believe that a man also has his part to play.

But those double standards can also be gratuitous. In teenage pregnancy: who gets the flack for it—the female or the male? Being found in a drunken stupor, a man is seen as simply drunk, but a female will be labeled as being uncouth. In regards to sex with an under-aged minor: who gets the most attention from it—

the adult male or the adult female? In single parenting, the male gets kudos for it, while with the female, it is commonplace. A man will no doubt make more money doing the same job as a woman. When a man cheats on his woman, the woman is accused of not doing her job and his actions are celebrated among other men. When a woman cheats on her man, she is accused of being a slut, and her man receives sympathy from others. When a woman sleeps around, she's a whore. When a man sleeps around, he is a hero. When an older woman dates a younger man, everyone wonders how she snagged him. When an older man marries a younger woman, there's not a second thought; except maybe, how much money is in his pocket.

Where Do Men Come From?

2

In the beginning of my marriage to my husband, it became clear to me that society has done a poor job of rearing our boys. I can say the same for our girls, and later I will, but for now, I'm going to begin with talking about boys and what has been done to undermine their future. This may appear to be a strong statement, but later I hope you'll start to understand where I am coming from.

My husband was not prepared for what it took to be married and have a successful union, nor was I. He was indeed a decent man, but he had no perception of what it took to be committed to someone inside of a marriage; the sharing of his things, time and patience, as well as remembering that he was married and no longer single when it came to making decisions that would affect not only him but both of us. I had to realize that I was married also and that it was okay to share responsibility of a task that had to be performed. Just because I was capable of hanging blinds in the window or hammering a nail in the wall didn't mean that I had to do it all. I had to be sensitive to how he wanted things arranged in the apartment. We had to compromise with each other about which of our things we had as single people, we would keep as a couple. I had to learn how to share my space and time, while not compromising my independence or spirit.

As I said, my husband had shown me that despite him having a sense of decency about himself, he was still selfish, insecure and immature at times. Women, we birth boys into the world, and we marry them. This is interesting to me because we basically fuck 'em up from the day they're born, during the rearing process, while dating them, and when we're married to them, all the way until the day they die. Let's face it; they didn't get to be the way they are by osmosis. Yes, ladies, we did it to them! We fucked them up!

I'm not insinuating that everything wrong in a relationship between a man and a woman is a woman's fault. I'm simply suggesting that we pay particular attention to how we deal with our men and raise our sons. A young girl that is fortunate enough to be raised in a healthy, loving, two-parent household will reap the benefits of having a father around. It will forever influence her relationships in the future with men. The same can be said of a young boy growing up in the same type of environment. What he sees and experiences will influence his relationship with women. But if for some reason a young boy does not have the benefit of having that healthy, loving two-parent home and is raised by a single mother or grandmother, etc., depending on the type of love he receives in his home, it can completely alter his perception of what it takes to be a ***real man***.

When a boy is born, everyone reveres him simply because he is a boy. He is born with the expectation that he will fulfill his duties as a man, but he is not raised with a true knowledge of what is expected of him. That's like teaching him to swim by throwing him in the water without any prior knowledge that he was going to be thrown in. He will either sink or swim, and that's not fair to our boys. Is it any wonder that they are ill-prepared for marriage, let alone relationships, when they've not been taught how to be in one? We teach them that real men don't cry or show any kind of emotion that will be viewed as making him look like a "punk." It's no wonder, either, that we have men walking up and down the streets with no jobs, drinking, abusing or beating their women and children. How can they compete with an expectation that they've not been fully made aware of?

Generally speaking, when we (men and women) learn that we are expecting a baby boy, we go nuts. We get so puffed up with the news, walking around with our chests stuck out as though we have done something more special than the creation of a healthy baby. There is absolutely nothing wrong with wanting to have that baby boy, but to not raise him to be a man is the unacceptable part in the equation.

Men have never had to fear being alone, without a woman. Whether or not they fulfill women's expectations is irrelevant, because some women will be happy just to have a man. She'll take him any way she can get him, sometimes even with the willingness to share him with someone else. Not only does a man not have to fulfill his duty as man with the woman in his life, he doesn't even have to do so with his children or the culture that continues to make excuses for his failure, and that's a shame.

I'm not saying that men are not judged, because they are, by the same society and women that have allowed them to be the way they are (child-like, disrespectful, abusive, etc.) all of their lives. The intention of the statement is to point out that if our men did not receive the appropriate nurturing they were supposed to receive as children and while growing up in the world, then maybe we need to start seeing it as our duty to set them straight as adults. I'm not talking about being their mothers or "changing" them (because it is impossible to change people, and anyone who believes that it's possible is deluding herself). What we can do is influence the change that they make in themselves by setting standards that we live by and holding them accountable for the life that we want with them.

When we as women complain about our men—such as comparing them to children or putting up with their unnecessary and immature behavior, while justifying it by saying, "You know how men are"—is an example of what I am talking about. It's like believing that there's no explanation or reason for sunlight, but you know there is one. I understand that you cannot change anything that you don't acknowledge. And why should you acknowledge that you have a problem with the man in your life? Especially when the problem is a common denominator among many women in relationships. One thing I have come to notice with many adults is that most of us don't like the feeling of being alone in a situation. We also don't like being in the minority and therefore we become a part of the "crab in the barrel" syndrome. But the only thing that can effect change is to first acknowledge that what you are going through is an unacceptable condition and being prepared for the fallout when others begin to challenge your view.

Even though I am not a man, I can still comment on the subject of why men are the way they are because of my own personal experience and from what I see happening around me. I can't speak from a man's perspective, but I can speak from the perspective of a mother who is raising a son to become a man and a woman who loves men.

Men have a lot of bad habits. They can be cheaters, abusers, users and liars, among other things. Where does that come from? Besides the fact that they do these things simply because they can, it can also be because it makes them feel good about themselves. Because they think it makes them look like a "big man" in someone else's eyes, or because they like being in control. But ultimately, I feel that it's because they don't know or want any better! I am not making excuses for them, just reiterating the fact that if they've never been taught what their expectations are or ought to be, how do they meet those expectations? And just because they don't know any better is no reason to put up with their bull! Being a liar, abuser, user or a cheater is not the problem—these are merely symptoms of a problem. They are the manifestations of something much bigger: being ill-prepared for life.

Relationships between father and son, and mother and son, can be very complex. A young boy may not have had the opportunity to know his father because his mother never disclosed the information (out of fear, indifference, hatred, etc. of the father), or because she doesn't know *who* the father is. For those boys who have fathers, the father may be around, but not involved in his son's life. This scenario plays a very significant role in the outcome of that boy. What kind of man he will become will then depend a lot on what kind of relationship that boy has with his mother.

It's not enough for a boy to have a father, or father figure. He also has to have a father (or father figure) who is willing to tell him the truth about what it takes to become a man, if *he* knows! There are a lot of boys raising boys, and by this I mean physically adult but emotionally child-like males. There is no way that an adult male who conducts his life without any responsibility can be successful in raising a man. (There are adult males out there who think the true measure of a man is to be able to produce children. Worse still, there are some who think that the true measure is one that can produce a boy!)

If a boy is fortunate enough to have an involved, responsible father or father figure, he will be blessed. It can, no doubt, have the greatest impact on how he will become a man. (I am a woman, and having my mother was the single most important thing I needed to grow up and become a woman.)

There are many myths that exist about what makes a man a real man. I have heard, firsthand, men saying that they've been told, while growing up, that a man is not a man unless he has more than one woman at any given time in his life, whether it is a wife and a mistress, or two or more girlfriends at a time. What kind of shit is this? Whatever it is, it's old! I realize there is still a lot of old-world thinking out there when it comes to molding our boys into men, and this is just an example of it. A responsible father would never tell a son this kind of silliness!

Women, think of the many men that have come into your life with these same jacked-up ideas about what it takes to be a man. You can't control what it is that they've come to believe is true. But it's time for us women (mothers, wives or friends) to influence change by not standing for such nonsense in our lives.

If a boy can't depend on his father, then of course, hopefully he'll have his mother to fall back on for support. Unfortunately, that relationship can either make or break that young boy. Many single mothers out there treat their young sons like they're the men in their lives. I'm not talking figuratively, I mean literally— such as creating a negative relationship by judging the women that he brings home, being a wedge between him and the woman in his life, or treating him like a baby and, worse yet, *spoiling* him!

I don't know about you, but in my opinion, when it comes to men and their habits, there's nothing worse than a spoiled adult male. What could he possibly know about what it takes to be a man… the sacrifices to be made in a successful relationship, for starters? In addition to that, there are women out there who are still feeding their boys the same jacked-up information of a man not being a real man unless he has more than one woman in his life. She gives him this faulty message with the things she says or by what he sees her going through every day with the man in her life.

We all want to be adored by the men in our lives, and some of us want it so bad that it is why many of us women have created an environment where the adoration can come from our sons. It may be messed up, but it is real. It can be very common with many of us women raising boys. And if he is a good-looking boy, all bets are off! How many parents go on and on bragging about all of the women their son can get? What is that?! If he hears it enough times, he will start to believe that it is all he has to offer, but in reality he is much more than a pretty face.

As I wrote before, boys, without the proper nurturing, can grow up into adult males without an iota of a clue about what it takes to be a man, let alone be in a relationship. Some men believe that the only requirement is being a good provider. I say, at least that's something, but it still isn't enough. A man is more than someone who can put food on the table. He is more than someone that is good in the bed. If he is to be considered a real man or the head of his household, then he should live his life by being an example to himself, his family and his community.

3

Where Do Women Come From?

As for where it began for us women, it also begins from child-hood as well. Just think of the many women whose name came from the fact that the parent(s) were hoping for a boy and there-fore never changed the name to reflect the birth of a female. I have heard that same story over and over again. Names like Tommie or Michael, to name a few. I must admit though, I think boy names for girls are cool.

Aside from name-calling, girls have the stigma of inferiority to boys from birth. We are treated as second-class citizens for not being born a male and are taught, even in the year 2011, that we are not complete without a man. That once we marry, we must submit unto our husband. We even have many cultures in today's modern society that continue to put the male gender on a pedestal and some that give incentives to having male babies while aborting female fetuses. I imagine that part of it is to preserve the family name and culture. But even so, none of it could be possible without us, the female! Talk about an oxymoron: what would happen to the women of the world if those practices were to continue?

Women, we don't know our own power! We have the power of procreation. We can make things happen when no one else can and out of nothing. We can multitask, and still be on point. With all of this power, it's amazing to me that we still don't know how powerful we truly are. WOW! We presently still have societies where women are to blame for not producing a male. That's an interesting concept; especially when it's the man that is responsible for the sex of the baby. But including this knowledge, I can't imagine anything that would make me want to make my beautiful female child feel unworthy.

I was very fortunate to be raised in the single-parent household that I grew up in. I didn't have a father growing up, but I did have a father figure; my maternal grandfather—not a blood relation. It was great to have him in my life, but it had a minimal impact on my development as a woman. I didn't have the experience of having a man around consistently as when there is a healthy two-parent household. What I did have was, and is, a wonderful mother. I am truly blessed.

This probably will be misunderstood, but I am going to say it anyway. I believe that part of my blessing probably came from *not* having a father around. The dysfunction in a two-parent home can come from the inconsistencies of having a mother and a father not being on the same page where their children are concerned.

In my own home, my husband will dismiss the misdeeds of our children and label them as just children being children. That may be true, but it doesn't mean that he is to take their actions as reason for doing nothing to correct them. How else will they learn the consequences of their actions? Another example of a dysfunctional two-parent household is when the parents are not mature enough to know that it is not cool to place a child in the middle of their battles, or to use them as leverage against each other. How awful!

My blessing also came from having a mother who didn't try to make up to me for not having a father around. She didn't treat me differently by feeling sorry for me, or herself, because of his absence. She didn't use it as a way of allowing me to get away with things, or as an excuse to let me have everything I wanted.

Overindulgence could possibly be one of the worst forms of child abuse. It is abusive because it is negligence. Just imagine, it's like being a rock star and no one ever says *no* to you. Children growing up in that type of situation can only be set up for a life full of disappointment and possibly failure. Because in the real world that I live in, you don't get things handed to you like that— on a platinum platter. You have to earn it to appreciate it. And in order to appreciate it, you have to have the experience of not always having things your way.

The first time my daughter had to change her sheets on the bed, I came into her room after about thirty minutes and found her on the floor whimpering. She was sitting there so distraught, holding on to the sheets like they were the source of her anguish; she's such a drama queen! The bed was still unmade and I asked her what was wrong. She said she couldn't get the fitted sheet on the mattress, even though I had previously shown her how to do it (so those tears of hers meant nothing to me.) I looked at her and told her to figure it out. There are adults who, as children, never had to figure "*it*" out. And as a result, still haven't figured "*it*" out! How many mothers or parents do you know who are still getting their adult children out of trouble by paying their bills or making excuses for their actions? Their parents made everything easy for them, and thus made them ill-prepared for life.

My mother never, ever made me feel that, in order to be happy in life, I had to have a man. I can remember when I was between thirteen and fourteen years old, she stopped seeing a man that had been in her life for several years. Weeks had gone by and I realized that I hadn't seen him, and she hadn't mentioned his name.

I went to her and asked if he'd ever be coming around again, and her response was *no*. I cried and asked her, "Was it something

I did wrong?" She responded to me with a smile on her face and understanding in her voice, "No, baby! It's not you; it just didn't work out. But Mama's okay, I'll be fine." As she spoke, she hugged me to reassure me.

Even though my mother never gave me the impression that I would be nothing without a man, I still thought it because of other things that I saw and heard. My mother, being a single parent without a high school education, was a poor mother. When he was around we had more in the house. He supported her, and lessened her struggle. And in my immature mind, I thought that as long as *he* was around, *we* would be better. I learned that my mother was willing to be alone and struggle rather than sacrifice herself or her beliefs just to have a man or things in her life.

As you can tell by now, my mother was an awesome teacher. She was exactly what I needed growing up, and I could go on and on, but that's for another book. So for now, I want to talk about other people's mothers. The relationships can be brutally dysfunctional. There are mothers out there who make bad decisions that affect their children's well-being. They may show love to one child and not the other, be jealous of their daughters, choose one child over another, do more for one than another, go on and on about how their children were a mistake or that she wanted a boy, and don't forget the ultimate: choosing a man over her children, whether he is the father or not.

Over the years, I have battled my own set of issues, one of them being overweight for most of my adult life. Now, when I first started looking to myself, to find out the reason behind the weight gain, I looked at whether or not the fact that I didn't have a father growing up was the reason. The answer was no! I found out that what my problem really was, was with my inability to not do things in excess. Whether it was spending money or eating, it always had to be the best and the most. While I am still dealing with my weight issues (and being somewhat successful at it), I have determined, however, that I did not and still do not have any father/daughter issues for the reason that, as I said earlier, my mother never allowed me to feel unworthy just because I didn't have a father. I didn't know pity for myself as an option.

There are many women out there who are dealing right now with this issue; debating whether their problems stem from the fact that their father was absent in some way or other (and this includes even some fathers who lived in the home, because a few think their only duty is to be present and not active). Some of you ladies may not know who your father is (maybe because your mother didn't know or she decided you didn't need to know). Maybe your father was disappointed in your being a girl (you may have heard this for most of your life and therefore, always felt unworthy), or he may have been abusive.

While it may be true that if our upbringing could have been white picket fenced-like, a lot of us could have turned out much different. It's amazing to me how many parents out there think that their only responsibility for raising their children is feeding, clothing and sheltering them. I would have to assume the obvious has never dawned on them, that the responsibility of raising children is much more than a notion. We actually have to teach them how to exist in the world, how to be productive, have a connection to themselves and the world outside of them so they are able to get along with others, and ultimately learn how to love themselves.

Our girls grow up experiencing many inconsistencies. They're told to love themselves and to accept themselves as they are. But when they watch television and look in the magazines, they are reminded over and over again that they are not good enough because of the way they look, live, or dress.

As women, we receive many messages that we're not good enough to compete with our younger generation, that men our own age are more interested in girls young enough to be our daughters. Knowing that this is true, why do we allow it to make us feel terrible about whom we are? We're not the ones with the problem; it's the people trying to tell us we have a problem that have one. Apart from having tighter skin and younger ovaries, a younger woman can't hold a candle to a more mature woman with a great sense of self. And anyway, only a *real* man would be interested in a *real* woman, just as a *real* woman would be interested only in a *real* man.

I can remember a time after losing about twenty pounds; this cute guy I knew said to me that I'd be good girlfriend material if I lost some weight (he didn't know that I had just recently dropped a few pounds.) Now mind you, I wasn't huge back then. I was probably wearing a size 10. But in comparison to young ladies my age at the time, who were wearing sizes 4-6, in my mind (because of people like him) I thought I was big. If only I could have appreciated myself more then.

Now as an adult woman, I would have told him to kiss my ass! Who the hell did he think he was, that he could tell me what was acceptable about me to him? I didn't have it in me to respond as I now would. I didn't have enough life experience to know better what to say or how to say it. Because I was still stuck in the land of sublime, I thought it was okay for him to say the things he said to me. But now, there is no confusion. I am fully able to express myself clearly and sometimes not so quietly.

I have heard all of my life to "*get your own.*" My mother constantly drilled it into my head that I was to get my education so I could have job security. It was so that I didn't have to depend on a man for whatever my needs were. Because if I had been dependent on a man for my needs, she knew that I wouldn't have been able to live a life of my own choosing. She worried that I would have sacrificed myself, or my beliefs, for "security."

I'm certain I am not the only woman to grow up hearing that. And there is nothing wrong with it. The problem is that with our education and job security, we are still taking care of (and catering to) our men! The irony is that our young women, on some level, are being groomed for a life that doesn't include a man, but young men are not groomed for a life without women! There is a vast difference between how girls and boys are raised. The double standards between the sexes start from the way we are raised. Girls have many expectations to live up to, but boys don't have as many, if any.

When I was pregnant with my first child, I wanted a girl. I had her name picked out long before she was a notion. I wanted her because I wanted to emulate the relationship that I have with my mother. Not only do I want to be close to her, I also want to teach her to be self-sufficient, independent and happy, just as she is. I want her to realize her potential in the world and how she can change it. I want to continue the cycle of teaching her how to independently care for herself. But I also want the same for my son.

On the flip side, there are some beautiful young women using their looks to get what they want. Some are encouraged to do so, and sometimes by the people closest to them, their mothers. I have witnessed it many times. A young daughter with "looks to kill" and the mother is *proud* of her offspring. The daughter has something the mother doesn't, or once had. So she lives her life vicariously through her daughter. That young lady, in turn, knows exactly how to get what she wants. There's nothing necessarily wrong with this; I say, use what you got. But she needs to know that nothing lasts forever, and she should be prepared for the consequences.

Because women set the tone for all relationships, we also determine the outcome of most relationships; our girls desperately need to know who they are. If we didn't have parents to teach us, we must teach ourselves. I believe one way to have a true sense of one's self is to have the courage to be *alone* because how can we know who we are if we've never taken the time to be alone? Being alone is probably something that even our parents were not able to do, or had to do—we are living in different times. I don't think, however, that we are meant to be alone forever, just in the meantime, in the between time. The desire for companionship is natural and necessary.

Being alone doesn't mean being lonely, because you can be surrounded by a wealth of people and still feel alone. The kind of alone I am talking about is being okay with being alone, with yourself. Not having to be in a relationship. I had a friend who would have a new boyfriend just after breaking up with one. I was exhausted trying to keep up with what man was current in her life. She didn't catch her breath in between relationships, nor did she learn a lesson from the breakups.

Learning to be alone is important. Having the ability to go out to a restaurant, or a movie, alone, for example. I did it often when I was younger, and single. I remember a guy asking me once, "What did you do today?" I told him that I went to see a movie and had dinner with myself. He asked, "Why?" I responded, "Because I wanted to." He gave me the impression that somehow my being alone, like that, was embarrassing, as though I should have been ashamed to be found sitting alone. He said the next time I got the urge to do something like that again to call him. I didn't see the sense in it. I did what I wanted to do. I enjoyed it. Maybe he thought that if I called him, he would get a free meal.

Some women, just as some men, have jacked-up ideas as well

about what makes a woman, a real woman. A real woman is more than someone who is capable of having children (and producing a son), keeping a house clean, cooking a meal, or keeping a man. None of it can be further from the truth. A real woman is someone who others can learn from. It takes a lot to break her. She is resourceful and can make anything happen, from nothing. She is the backbone of our society, and therefore our families, and we need to get her back!

Parenting

As I wrote earlier, having children is more than a notion and when it comes to raising them, they deserve so much from us, probably much more than we, as individuals, can give them. It is not about how many things they have, how popular they are, or where they live.

Parenting is the hardest thing that I have EVER, OR WILL EVER do, but I am up for the challenge because my children didn't ask to be here. They were my choice and my blessing. If I earned a billion dollars, it will not compare to the feelings of joy and overwhelming love that I have for my children. Or to have someone compliment me on something my child has done to show that they have been raised to have manners and be respectful of others, especially their elders.

It's so hard raising children now in this year 2011, and it will only get harder. There are still women out there having children that they shouldn't be having. Many children are raising themselves and their siblings, and they don't live in Third World countries. It's hard raising children, because as a parent you can't afford to be immature, lazy, inconsistent or unavailable. They need more than the usual—food, clothing and shelter. They also need to be taught things, not just from an academic standpoint. Growing up for children is also about social, psychological and physical development. Most of it won't be taught in school. And even if it is, parents are still responsible for its interpretation. As parents, we are ultimately responsible for our children's overall well-being.

We need to start paying attention to our children and not making excuses for their actions, just as we make for our own and the man in our lives. We need to pay attention to our children so that we know who our children are. When they come home from school at the end of the day and they're in a foul mood, are you going to ignore it or investigate it? My children should be coming in the house with smiles on their faces. They don't work anywhere! What problems could they have in their little lives to change who they are, when they walk through the doors at the end of the day?

You had better investigate, because there can be no telling what is bothering your children. In their little lives, everything is packed with drama. My daughter can come home and be upset because another kid may have not wanted to play with her at school, despite her best efforts to get that kid's attention. But I want to make sure that is all that is ailing her. I am aware how children can hide so much. But I also believe that if we have a connection with our children and pay particular attention to them, we can help them with some of the most challenging situations they can be faced with.

We have to protect them from predators, those living both in and out of the home. When I was a little girl, about eight or nine years old, I was walking down the street holding my younger (by one year) cousin's hand. There was a man in a pickup truck. He gestured for me to come over. I did. He was sitting there holding and playing with his swollen penis. We didn't talk about stranger danger to the tenth degree back then in our house, and we should have. Not that things like that didn't happen back then. It's just that nowadays they don't simply show their private parts, they abduct!

When I was in the fifth grade, one day after school was over and most everyone was gone, the janitor gestured for me to go over to where he was. I did. He guided me into the janitor's storage closet and lifted me from behind, around my abdomen. My feet were no longer touching the floor. I remember his breathing, hard, on my neck. By this time my pulse was racing with the thought of what was to come. He put me down quickly when he thought he heard someone coming toward the room. As soon as he put me down, I ran from that room so fast that it would have made your head spin. I was embarrassed and didn't tell anyone at the time because I thought it was *my* fault!

When I was a few years older, there was an old man from the neighborhood who was very handy. He was at our house to fix the kitchen sink for my mother. Everyone was in the room. He was standing in front of me (facing me) and he lightly squeezed my nipple between his forefinger and middle finger. I immediately removed his fingers, covered my breast with my hand and then, quickly walked away. I didn't utter a sound to imply that I had been insulted, or violated. I never spoke a word about it until I became an adult. Not one person, absolutely no one, saw what he had done. And there was a room full of people present! Again, I didn't say anything because I was embarrassed and somehow thought it was my fault because I should have known better. I know now that if I had said something, someone's ass would have been kicked. I also could have spared another child from having the same thing, if not worse, happen to them.

There are people in my life who think I am too overprotective of my children. My experiences, even though I was not sexually molested, were experience enough for me to know that I have to monitor not only my children's behavior, but also the behavior of those who would potentially have any alone or private time with them. It was easy for me to hide what had been done to me, because in my child's mind, it was my fault. But what if I had been molested? Would I have acted out? Would my grades have been affected? Would I have become withdrawn?

We have to protect our children from themselves. I don't know about you, but no matter how smart I thought I was growing up, I probably didn't really start to learn who I was until I was as least thirty years old. So, the parents who gave permission for their sixteen-year-old daughter to marry her high school track teacher (who was at least forty years old; it was a story I saw on *Good Morning America*) did her a disservice by giving her what she wanted after she had what basically amounted to a tantrum in order to get her way. It may appear that I am being judgmental, especially since I possibly don't have all of the facts, but they didn't protect her from herself. I think about how often children are victims of crimes because they didn't heed their parents' warnings or advice about dangerous situations. We can never give up on our children. When one thing doesn't work, then we have to find something else. We have to stay on them like white on rice.

Sometimes children have to be protected from the very people that are raising them, their parents. You cannot know how many times I have heard a person make the excuse about how spoiled their child is, and the fact that the other parent is to blame for it. My husband told me that he personally witnessed a woman trying to keep from looking embarrassed when her four-year-old daughter tried to clock her. I heard that same woman saying how she can't do anything with her own daughter. That she's her daddy's child, and that it's because of him that she is that way. Parenting is not a joke! If you want well-rounded children, you have to put forth the effort!!! I have seen women put forth more effort to get and keep a man. In comparison, that's a joke.

I have spoken a lot about us women and our parenting skills, but let me say something about men and their parenting skills. There are some really great fathers out there. My husband is not only a decent person, but he is a decent father as well. He can be inconsistent and a little on the lazy side, but his intentions are good. But believe me when I say, he gets no pat on the back from me where my children are concerned for his inconsistency and laziness.

He does get a pat on his back from me for being available for his children. He no doubt loves his children and spends a lot of time with them, probably more than I when it comes to the quantity. He takes them many places with him and feels insulted when he hears someone comment on how nice it is to see him "babysitting" his children. His usual response to the offending query is more of a question than a statement, "How can I babysit what is mine?"

Just as there are good fathers, there are some fathers who, even when they are in the home, are spiritually disconnected and physically unavailable. How many times have you had to run errands and your husband wants you to take the child or children with you so that he can watch TV? How many times, while out in public with your family, are you the one who has to go to the bathroom to change the baby's diaper because he won't? How many times have you seen a child cry out for comfort while in their father's presence? He does nothing to console the child, not even look at the child, to show his sympathy for what *his* child is going through? And how responsible are you as the mother that in some way caused that disconnection between father and child? It may have not been intentional, but you did it because you thought you could do it all, or because you thought you could do it all better than him. Whatever the reason may be, think about your possible contribution to it.

When my first child, my baby girl, was born, I was paranoid about everything. I remember my husband trying to encourage me to get some sleep in the guest bedroom. He told me to go to sleep and that he would sleep with the baby (in the bed with him). I couldn't rest because all I could think about was him rolling on top of her, or her falling off the bed and getting wedged between the bed and the nightstand! I had to let that go! I was driving myself crazy, so I stopped my behavior (i.e., my insanity) because I was determined not to raise her alone. What would've been the point of having her father there; only to be a warm body? For most women, mothering is natural. But fathering may not come as easily; it may have to be experienced by the man, so don't take the opportunity of experiencing this away from him.

Getting back to us parenting our children, we have to learn how to have effective communication between our children and ourselves. Communication with them doesn't start when they are teenagers and out of your control. We have to start by having a healthy relationship with them from the time they are born, when they become toddlers and eventually, independent, school aged teenagers, young men and women, and mature adults.

Stop trying to be their friend and letting them run things. It makes no sense that someone that is not able to pay a bill can control a household. Even if that child were earning the household income, they still need some rules, boundaries and guidance. Children not only need discipline, but they want it. Imagine a three-year-old holding an adult hostage; that's ludicrous! But that's essentially what is happening in some households. Ladies, man-up and stick your chest out and take care of your children. The decisions that you make for your children will not always be popular with them, but who cares? The point is to prepare them for a world outside of their home. Even as toddlers, they have to learn how to interact with others. **They can be told no**! They will learn that even if they hear the word no, it doesn't mean they aren't loved. They will one day soon find out that life goes on, and that things will be okay even though they haven't gotten their way.

Children are different from one another. My younger sister and I are as different as night and day, and that's perfectly okay. How many times have you heard the comment made about how different two children are that came from the same household? Personally, I've heard it many times. First of all, my sister and I are two different people. Second, we have two different personalities. And third, we have two different sets of needs. Many children are unfortunate because they grow up in a situation where they are constantly being compared to another sibling. Parents have to realize that what works for one child may not be what works for another.

My daughter has the perception that her baby brother gets preferential treatment over her, to be more specific, that we love him more than her. That's outrageous! I know it's what she thinks because I asked her, when I saw that she seemed to have an insatiable appetite for my affection and attention. To love my son more than her would be impossible, but she doesn't understand that right now. Of course, I explained to her that it is not the case. She doesn't realize, even though it has been explained to her, that she received the same attention from us as he does now when she was his age (if not more). When she was a baby, it was just her. There were no other children around to divert our attention from her. She had the mother lode of attention. She was our firstborn, the baby we prayed for. She had the latest and greatest of everything, and she was an itty-bitty baby girl. Her wardrobe was bigger than mine; it was absurd.

The two of them are completely different. She is always in

trouble, and he hates being in trouble. She is all girl; he is all boy. I explained to her that they will always be raised differently, but loved the same. It's another thing I don't expect her to understand right now, but she eventually will. They are two completely different little souls. They deserve to have the individual attention that is necessary to help them blossom into beautiful, productive human beings.

No matter how "good" we think we are as parents, we will be a disappointment to our children and ourselves at times, because we can't always be on point. The most important thing is to *try* to do the right thing when it comes to your children. There are no guarantees in life. You can do the best you can, and your children may still go astray. But hopefully, with a lot of prayer and support, they will come back to their roots, and to the people who, ideally, will always be there for them.

Know that if your child is getting into situations like becoming truant in school, doing drugs, getting in and staying into trouble, these are not the problem—they are the symptoms of a problem. When things deviate from the norm, or our perception of what's normal, we want to put our children in a box and place labels on them. And that's what we are doing with our children.

You don't know how many times I have heard someone say, in the presence of his or her child, that he is so "*bad!*" It's a self-fulfilling prophecy. How many times do you think a child has to hear something like that before they start to believe that it's true, and exhibit behavior to make it so? It is our duty as mothers to help correct the problem if it can be fixed. We can never give up on our children. Like I said before, when one thing doesn't work we have to try something different. Because remember, no matter what a man thinks he contributes to a child's life, it is nothing in comparison to what a mother brings to the table.

Women Are From Jupiter
Men Are from Uranus

5

There are many differences between men and women, besides the obvious physical differences. But with our many differences, there are many similarities. One similarity is being human. We both have the same bodily functions and emotions; the only difference is the way our emotions are manifested. Women, we cry, bitch and moan, while men become liars, users, abusers and cheaters, as I said earlier.

There are some so-called experts out there who will lead us to believe that love is a game. Like for example, if a man takes you to a movie of his choosing, and you didn't like it, you shouldn't say so because he may take it as an attack on his male ego. What the hell is that? You can't know how many times I have heard from other women's mouths that they want to tell their men something, but they have to take into account their male egos.

It's an oxymoron that a man can be considered strong, a man's man, a manly man, but you have to consider not bruising his ego. Just think about it for a second: can't a real man handle the truth? I am not talking about the truth in saying something that would require a little tact, kindness and sensitivity to the information he is about to receive. But more like the truth in telling him that you didn't like the color he chose to paint a wall, sharing dialogue about the movie the two of you saw and your differing opinion on that or any other subject. Or is a woman not to have an opinion, ever? It is my opinion that it should require a lot more than this to emasculate a man. And if I were wrong, that would be a problem!

It would be a problem because in the relationship, the woman will always be on guard, trying to protect his feelings. And on some level she will be unable to feel comfortable being who she needs to be in order to be happy in the relationship. How can she be happy if she can't be honest enough to say how she feels? She can't! She will be too busy making sure that his feelings are nurtured. Because what she wants will be secondary to what his feelings may be, because of fear of how he will react to the information she wants to share with him.

If a man doesn't call, who wrote the rule that says you can't call him first? That's playing games, again. If a woman sleeps with a man on the first date, does that make her easy? Maybe. Or is that merely an excuse a man would use not to follow up with her? I believe it is a combination of both and more. Because in my mind, a real man would make the choice to tell a woman what is on his mind and how he feels, and would never use a woman for her body and then not call because he wants her to believe that he thinks she's easy. If a man were truly interested in a woman he slept with after knowing her for a short time, he'd accept that there was chemistry between the two of them, instead of believing the worst of her—that she does the same thing with other men that she meets. But if he were no longer interested in her, he would use the excuse that "she's easy" as a way out. Just like a woman, when it comes to a man, if there's something that he wants, there's almost nothing that can be said or done to change his mind.

Another huge difference between men and women is that most of us women become invested in a man too quickly. I can remember when I was younger and I'd be interested in a guy, I could envision my entire life with him in it; until he revealed himself as an asshole. There's nothing wrong with that, in and of itself. But there are women out there whose perspective of a relationship changes from the first date or sexual encounter.

I know women who are unable to separate sexual intimacy from having a relationship. They've convinced themselves that they are unable to keep themselves from falling in "love" with someone that they've just had sex with. I remember a college friend saying that she wanted me to meet her boyfriend. I wasn't aware that she had one! She told me then that they had had sex with one another and therefore they were "boyfriend and girlfriend."

It is nothing new that men don't equate sexual intimacy with having a steady relationship. I am a woman, and I never understood why we women do. A girlfriend of mine had a blind date set up for her by a good friend and she was so worried about how he looked and the consequences of it. I asked her why she was so stressed out about it. I told her it wasn't like she was going on a date to get married, and that she should accept it for what it was, enjoy the date, and if the situation became unbearable, end it early. She looked at me with a relieved expression because she had never thought of it that way. That *she* had a choice. She had not met him and already she was planning her life with him.

Men can use the promise of marriage as a way to keep us in line. My old boyfriend, for example, had me where he wanted me because of it. He always made references to me that we would someday be married. What the hell was that? In these situations, men have us how they want us by continuing to have the benefits of a married couple, without being married, like perhaps doing his laundry and cooking his meals. Doing these things shouldn't be a problem for you as long as it is what you want and not what he wants, and also if the relationship is reciprocal. If he talks about the day that you'll be married, but never commits to a date, you may have to eventually come to the conclusion that he is all talk.

For the lady who wants to be married, when the day arrives that he asks for your hand in marriage, I hope that it is not shared on a day that is special or significant. Valentine's Day is okay! But imagine being given an engagement ring as a gift as though it's you, not him, who wants to be married. I would be more impressed if he popped the question on his birthday or on Christmas Day, as if he wants this as a gift for himself. He would ask you if you would do him the extreme honor of giving him the gift he has always wanted, you! Isn't that special?

Why is a man the center of a woman's universe and why is marriage the ultimate prize? Did we somehow give them that impression? I believe so; that is why many marriage proposals are made on particularly special days. If my husband had given me an engagement ring and asked for my hand in marriage as a Christmas or birthday gift to me, he would have been in big trouble. This is my feeling on the subject—my perspective. Maybe there are some women out there who consider a promise of marriage as a gift. Yuck!

Marriage, for me, is a constant reminder of how different men and women are. My husband constantly challenges me as an individual, and as a woman, in our marriage. I have to regularly defend myself against his perception of what I should be in the marriage, although I don't have to so much anymore as I did in the beginning. Still, I do this more than I should have to; even if that means once a year.

Very early in our marriage we lived in an apartment on the second floor; the top level. One day, we were bringing in the groceries and it was a lot of stuff, so we needed to make many trips to bring in all the bags. Needless to say, we were both spent, not only from the shopping, but also from getting the packages inside. Once the last package was placed in the kitchen, my husband swiftly went into the living room, got the remote control, sat down and turned the TV on. No big deal. I thought he was just going to see what was on the television and come back, but minutes went by and I realized he wasn't coming.

I went into the living room and asked him if he was going to help. He let out a big sigh, and came back into the kitchen and said to me, "The difference between you and me is that you do it when it needs to be done, and I do it when I feel like it." Immediately when he said it, he knew what he said was wrong, I could see it in his eyes, but he couldn't take it back; it was already in the universe. What I heard him saying was that he didn't care if the house was messy or if the dishes needed to be cleaned, etc. Not me, I like my house to look neat and clean, albeit lived in, and for things to be in their place. But he could walk past the dirty dishes in the sink for weeks and not have a second thought about it until he needed a clean one.

Women are very maternal, sometimes to a fault. We complain about how our men act like children, but we treat them like children. However, the only people we should be mothering are the little people in our lives. My healthy, self-reliant husband does not need me to speak or do for him as a mother would. If he does, then I don't need him. I am a handful enough on my own, not to mention my children.

I am a nurse by trade. On a fairly consistent basis, when I have a man as a patient, it is his wife who is able to give a detailed history on him. That would be okay if he were in a coma. But he is alert and oriented, and when a question is asked of him, he looks at his wife for guidance. She answers, with authority and pride, because he depends on her for so much. How sweet! I am so unimpressed by the fact that she knows her husband better than he knows himself. She probably knows him better than she knows herself! How sad!

Once I was at a doctor's visit with my husband, and the question was asked of him what his allergies were. He had the nerve to look at me like I was going to answer for him. I looked right back at him like he was crazy. He thought it was okay for me to answer for him because I am the nurse in the family. But he needs to take charge and responsibility for his own body and health. What is he going to do when I am not with him? Call me on my cell phone to get an answer about himself? I don't think so.

When it comes to the approach by which we handle our household duties, my husband and I are as different as night and day. Remember the comment that he made to me about the difference between us—that I do it when it needs to be done, and he does it when he feels like it? Well, I have never let him forget it. It's wrong, I know, but I can't help it. He makes it so damn easy by being so typical.

My husband wouldn't agree with me, but he has a tendency to not pick up around the house on a regular basis. If he mops the floor, it's because it has become unbearable to walk on. If he cleans the tub, it's because he has become aware of the ring around it that has been there for at least two weeks, because I refused to clean it. The trash could be overflowing, but he will only take it out if it's time for the trash pickup, if he has noticed there is an ant problem or else, if I remind him to do it. I remember saying to him once that the trash needed to be emptied and his reply was, "But I put it out yesterday!" Like he didn't realize that it has to be done every day. Furthermore, it doesn't matter the shambles the house could be in, he will go outside and keep those damn cars CLEAN! But outside of the reasons mentioned, he will do some serious housecleaning when he is expecting company. Isn't that funny; he cares about what others see, not what he has to see on a daily basis.

I will admit, though, that in the beginning of our marriage, I made things very easy for him. I thought it was the thing you do when you love someone. I used to work myself into a frenzy to keep the house looking decent. I have tried unsuccessfully to get my husband to partner with me in keeping the house neat. He says he does, but he doesn't understand that my goal would be to have our home to look decent, every day—not just when he feels like it, when it becomes noticeable to him, or when people are coming over.

I made things easy for him in the beginning because I wanted to feel needed by him. I wanted to be indispensable to him. Indispensable? Is that what we women have become? It was cute at first. Now it is exhausting and way too time-consuming. When my husband didn't do things that needed to be done, I would do them. When he didn't remember things, I would remember them for him. If he wanted something, I made sure that it was perfect!

It started after our daughter was born; I was not only caring for her, but I was also caring for him and lastly, caring for myself. Very soon after that, things started to change for me. I became aware of the monster of my creation, my husband. He became a man that depended on me for waaaaaay too much. I was his personal assistant. If he wanted a phone number, he would ask me. If he wanted to remember how to get somewhere, he would ask me. I became his personal database. It got so bad that I began to wonder how in the hell did he function when I was not around. I found out that he could function fine without me. That was when I realized what I had done and decided I no longer wanted to be indispensable for him, but for myself.

I realize my husband needs me. He needs me to love, support

and encourage him. He also needs me for the things that he can't do on his own, like having his children, cooking a meal, or altering his pants, etc. Believe it or not, he can do all of it except the have children part; for that, I was indispensable. I'd like to see him try and accomplish that on his own. Even if he could, he would perish with the pain and discomfort.

I don't need to have him dependent on me for everything out of fear that he could find someone else to do it for him. I have my own life. If I were to start living his life for him, then I couldn't be my own person. My happiness in our marriage does not come out of a need to feel that he can't do anything without me. How could I have ever become the person that I was meant to be for me, if I were to become the person he needs me to be for him? I could not have!

Commitment

6

As a young woman, I believed I would never marry. I was completely at peace with the notion. I was okay with it because I grew up thinking that *all* men cheat. I bought into the concept because it was all I knew. I was a teenager when I saw a male family member driving around in his car with a woman that was not *his* wife, and I wasn't confused about who or what she was. I also knew it was not to be talked about.

A good friend of mine came to me once, crying that she found condoms in her boyfriend's wallet (knowing that they didn't use them). She confronted him about the situation and he was honest with her. I said to her, "What's the big deal; all men cheat!" I said it with a straight face and I meant it; I really did. How she felt about the betrayal was of no matter to me because I couldn't understand why she didn't know what I knew; that it was an acceptable behavior. How silly of me!

My experiences, what I witnessed and heard from others, led me to believe that it was impossible for men to be faithful, especially Black men. But one day, while in the park studying for an upcoming exam with my friends, I saw a family: a pregnant Black woman, a Black man and their toddler son. I couldn't help but notice them. They seemed like an anomaly; they actually seemed happy.

It really wasn't the woman I noticed. I thought most women were happy to have a man who was willing to be with them (that was during a time when I believed that the man in the relationship was the prize.) What I really saw was that the *man* seemed content with where he was in his life. It appeared as though *he* was happy with the life that *he* had chosen; he wasn't being held at gunpoint against his will to portray the faithful, happy husband.

It was then that I started to change my perception of what it meant to me to be in a committed relationship. I realized that it *was* possible to find a man who was willing and able to be committed and happy in a relationship. Now, I have no idea about what the "park man" was really like. He could have been an asshole for all I knew, but he gave me hope. I began to understand that it was all about choices, the choice to be happy and committed in a relationship. So, I made the choice then that if I were to find a man I wanted to share my life with, he would have to be committed to me; no exceptions!

Even though I knew that I would only be in a committed relationship, not until I got married did I understand that marriage and commitment *do not* go hand in hand. They should, but they do not. The world is full of people, mostly women, who appear to believe that marriage is the be all and end all of a woman's existence. *Well, it is not!* There are plenty of people out there who are married and, at the same time, not committed to anyone. Not to their spouses or children. And that's a shame.

Marriage is **hard** work! The commitment that my husband and I have to one another and to our children is something that we chose. We work hard to maintain it, *every day*, not when the feeling hits us. Our being committed to one another didn't come about because we are married, or because we have children, but because we needed and wanted to be so.

How many people do you know, especially men, who are married in name only? The reason could be because it sounds good in theory or looks good on paper. It could also be because it's the thing to do when you get to a certain age, or because they don't want to grow old or be alone. Who knows? But why would he want to be married if he's going to be out in the strip clubs every weekend? By the way, I'm not opposed to my husband going from time to time and maybe taking me along! Why does a man get married if he's got to hang out with his "boys" all the time, or has an insatiable need to go clubbing on a frequent basis?

Dr. Phil is right when he says, "We teach people how to treat us." Knowing this statement is true, then, most women have taught their men that it is okay to not be committed to her or his children, by accepting their men's behavior.

If every woman in the world would change her behavior in terms of what it means to be in a committed relationship, it would greatly change the outcome of most relationships. It won't happen, but I can be optimistic. I remember when I would go into a relationship expecting the worst, but hoping for the best. What the hell did that mean? I was young, and I was only trying to be prepared for the failure of a relationship because of my preconceived notions about men and cheating. It was ignorant of me to start in a relationship expecting it to fail. I have learned to go into something expecting nothing but the best, because it is what I deserve. If it doesn't work out, then either it was not as expected, or less than what I deserve. I will see *it* for what it is. I will move forward and learn from the experience so that I can get that much closer to what I need and want.

I want to take a moment to clarify something. As I go on, I will be using the words "ignorant" and "stupid" a few times and I want to give my definition for the two. I want to clarify because the word "ignorant" has a negative connotation, but what it means is basically "being unaware." Being ignorant is when you don't know, and you don't know that you don't know, basically not knowing any better. It has nothing to do with educational status—it has everything to do with knowledge from experience. I am an educated woman, but I am ignorant of things that are outside of my own personal circle of knowledge. "Stupid," on the other hand, is when you're wrong and you know it, because you know better. But don't get it twisted, because some people play ignorant. When they have to pretend not to know any better, actually, they're playing stupid.

My past misunderstanding that all men cheat came by word of mouth from both the women and men in my family. Infidelity was talked about as a fact of life. And as I have said before, there are men out there who teach their sons that a man is not a man unless he has two women. The sad part is that mothers are teaching their boys the same thing.

We have all heard how important a man's monetary contribution to his family is, but what is required of a man to be committed is not talked about enough. A man being committed to his family far extends past paying the bills and further, commitment to family is not always about fidelity. Commitment is not all about what someone has to feel for you. We have to be committed to ourselves and to the people that depend on us as well. But above all, being committed to someone also means knowing the worst of someone, yet still loving them in spite of their imperfections. That's commitment!

Infidelity

Contrary to popular belief, all men are not dogs! Even though I haven't met every man in the world, my husband is my inspiration for believing that statement is true. He happens to be one of the good guys. So it is my belief that there are many more men, in existence, than my husband, who are fully willing to be in a loving, committed, monogamous relationship with a woman.

I could talk for days about the subject of why it is that men cheat. But whatever the excuses made for it, ultimately it comes down to one thing—because they can. As women, we take on the responsibility of the many things that go wrong in our lives. But because I know better, this is one thing I won't take ownership of, if it were to happen to me. I should never say "never," but I'm pretty damn sure of this! I have experienced being cheated on, and it was not what I was or wasn't doing that made him do it. When a man cheats, it has more to do with him, the cheater, than the one being cheated on. He may use the excuse that he's a man and that it's in his nature, whatever the hell that means. He may say it is because his woman doesn't give it to him often enough or the way he likes it, that he is no longer attracted to his woman. Or he could use the fact that "it" has been handed to him on a "platinum" platter. But whatever the reason, he has to take responsibility for his wrongdoing and you have to hold him accountable for it.

Women, we get a raw deal in the area of being cheated on. My husband and I had a discussion once about a man that we knew. He was a "faithful" cheater. There wasn't anything that he wouldn't screw. He'd screw it as long as it wasn't nailed down! Now, the people who knew him and his wife whispered behind her back, as though somehow his cheating had some reflection on her. In my opinion, the extent of their expression should have been non-judgmental and supportive of her when the time arose. But instead, what happened is that those same people judged her for having a philanderer for a husband. They expressed it with amusement mixed with apathy in their judgment because they knew that she was aware of his ways.

I told my husband that his view of the situation was offensive to me, as a woman. He didn't understand what I meant at first, so I asked him why did he think that the fact the guy was cheating had anything to do with her, the wife? She was being judged because she stayed with him, but still, what does that have to do with her? The basis of their relationship is the basis for many relationships, and how dare someone criticize her for being in a situation that they've probably found themselves in? The only difference between her relationship with her husband and that of others is that many cheating relationships stay in the closet and their dirty laundry stays private.

I have been the woman who was cheated on and I've been the woman used to cheat with—and neither of these situations have an advantage. I dated someone that I thought was single. But come to find out, I was the one that he was cheating with.

I was there in his apartment sleeping (well, I might add), when someone knocked on the door at approximately 3 a.m. He got up to answer the door and I heard some muffled sounds—back and forth (fast) talking. Then I heard fast footsteps coming toward the bedroom. It was her! She made her way to the bathroom and turned the light on, and she turned to see me lying in the bed with my naked body covered with the sheets. I made eye contact with her and I saw her pain. I was sad for her because I thought that someone had to win, and good thing it was me. How immature was I to think that it was about him being some prize and that I had won. What I should have been was offended that he started a relationship with me without completely severing the one he had with her.

Within one year of this relationship, I became the one being cheated on. It's funny how things go. You have to be careful; the same way you get a man is sometimes the same way someone else can, too. And that's exactly what happened. Even though I didn't "steal" him from his previous girlfriend, I should have recognized his actions as a potential pattern and been wary of it. But remember, I thought I had won.

What that experience taught me was that it's important to get to know people when you're starting a relationship with them by paying attention to their habits. I should have known better. Once she left, we spoke about it. He sat there with his head hung low in his hands to get sympathy from me; he was pretending to be so sad. But who was he sad for: her, because he didn't want to hurt her like that, or himself, because he was found out?

He said that he had tried to break it off with her and that *she* was having a hard time letting go. I didn't believe it when he said it to me. I saw the look in her eyes. It was pain! If what he said were true, then it would not have happened the way it had. It was him who didn't want to let her go; he wasn't sure of how I would work out for him. He probably wouldn't have broken it off at that time if it weren't for her seeing what she saw. He had to make a decision and I was in season at that moment.

I didn't believe it was true when he said to me that he was trying to break it off with her; a few weeks earlier I had spotted her driving *his* car. Yes, I had seen another woman driving *my* man's car! So I asked him about it and he said that they were still "friends" and that she needed a way to get around in order to take care of some errands. That is not what I saw. I saw a woman comfortably driving her man's car. But I allowed myself to believe what he told me.

Ladies, let me tell you something: if something doesn't make sense, then it's not right. If it walks like a duck, quacks like a duck, looks like a duck, it's a duck. What happened to me was a sign that I didn't heed. If you come home one day and your home is empty of furniture and things, or your man tells you that he wants a separation or divorce, don't pretend like you didn't have any warnings. There are always signs. They are not always the flashing neon type. They can be as subtle as minor changes in his attitude or daily habits. This is not for you to be paranoid with everything that happens, but just for you to take steps to know the person that you've committed yourself to.

You know how men can be; they'll say that your actions drove them to cheat. Being a cheater has more to do with the cheater rather than the person being cheated on. Like I said, as women, we are responsible for so much that we even take ownership of the fact that we've been cheated on. I would be more interested in why a man cheated on me, rather than the fact that he cheated. Being cheated on isn't always about the usual excuses made for it. I once thought that if a man loved me or was committed to me, then, he wouldn't cheat. I still believe that. But I've come to realize that love is different for different people and some people's definition of what it means to be committed is different as well.

As I mentioned before, we live in a society that judges a woman for her man's infidelity. Just like the guy mentioned earlier, I remember another guy I worked with. He was a walking *HO!* He was married with a small child. His wife had to be aware of it because he didn't seem to do anything to conceal his cheating ways. I heard every comment you could think of, most of it concerning how his wife was the fool to allow something like that to go on under her nose. Well, if she was a fool, then what was he?

He thought he was some kind of stud muffin and was seemingly celebrated in his circle of friends. I suppose it made him feel like a man because he was successful in proving his point; that he could get some new pussy. There were many women who were willing to give it to him because they had nothing better to do. If they did, they would have been doing it. I had no respect for him and as a woman, I was insulted because it was his wife that was being judged for his infidelity. While his actions, as I said, were celebrated, she was wrongly judged. But she was not an innocent bystander in all of this. She was no longer innocent from the time she became aware of his "cheating ways." What she was accountable for, was allowing herself to be in a relationship with a man who didn't respect her enough to leave her if she was not the one he wanted to be with. Because she had a choice, but I guess she made it!

If my man were found to be a cheater, I'd try and keep it in perspective by being more concerned with why he cheated rather than worry about the fact that he cheated. If your man cheats on you because you are not able to perform your "wifely" duties, what does that make him? Selfish, immature, stupid and insensitive! If your man cheats on you with a woman who gave it to him the way he likes it and you don't, what does that make him? Selfish, immature and stupid! If your man cheats on you because, at the moment, you're not speaking or giving it up to him as an expression of your disappointment about the current state of your relationship and his lack of doing what is necessary to change the state of the relationship, what does that make him? Selfish, immature and stupid!

When I am pissed at my husband for something, I am *not* able to be intimate with him. When I was younger, it was easier to separate my need for sexual intimacy and being disappointed in my mate. My life experiences have made it impossible to separate the two; I am a few years older and sharing my life with someone. I am unable to separate them because part of the intimacy that is shared, between my husband and me, can be as simple as him putting out the trash without my having to remind him to do it. That's how he shows me love!

So when he does something, knowing full well it will make me angry, he also knows that it will take me more than a minute to get over my feelings of disappointment, and therefore more than a minute to be intimate with him. He has tried to use "threats" of him cheating because of it. Like he thought I could be bullied into having sex with him out of fear that he would be "forced" to find someone else to have his "needs" satisfied!

He would say to me, "I know why men cheat on their wives!" as though if I heard that, it would make the threat seem more real. But I feel that if you're man enough to say some shit like that to me, be man enough to hear what I have to say. Because I say what I mean, and I mean what I say. My response was, "Oh really! Are you threatening me? Tell me now. 'Cause if you decide to go somewhere else, you had better be sure it's who you want to get it from for the rest of your life, because I will shut it down!"

Using that type of threat was his way of trying to control me. He would be so upset with me, but I couldn't have cared less. It's playing games, and I have no time for games. If he knows that he has done something to make me, the person he claims to love, upset, but expects me to be okay with his actions, why is he upset when he doesn't get what he wants, when he knows how I will react? As long as we've been together, he knows exactly which buttons to push, but he'll be playing that game by himself!

I realized that the threat was "empty." Even if it wasn't, I won't be bullied into doing something that I don't want to do. I can't perform an adult act with someone who would act like a toddler. And I would never put his needs over my feelings. Had the threats been something that he made good on, then he would have not been the man that I expected him to be. I would have acknowledged it, and dealt with it. But anyway, I don't have time for that kind of silliness.

Whether a man's cheating is an example of his stupidity, immaturity, insensitivity or selfishness, the end result is still because he could and he knew you would stand for it—even when the result of his infidelity is your pain and disappointment. But what about women; why do we cheat? I am a woman and still I don't know why some women cheat. Is it because he's not giving it to you the way you want it, because you want to pay him back for cheating on you, or just because you can? Whatever the reason, it still ain't right!

If the reason for your infidelity is because you think that you're in love with another man, remember that the grass is not always greener on the other side. The grass still has to be mowed. I guarantee it, once you become involved with that man, you'll find out something you didn't know about his ass, and you'll wonder: what the hell was I thinking?! If the reason for your infidelity is because you no longer love your man, then break up with him. Why complicate things by starting something that has the possibility of changing who you are, and not necessarily for the better, with possible negative consequences?

There are many people who end up in relationships they shouldn't be in. How many women do you know who are in relationships with people because they thought they couldn't do any better? I know of a woman being in a relationship with a man, but she cheated on him with what she thought was her ideal man, only to have *both* relationships fail. Because she feared being alone, she cheated herself and wasted time with a man that she did not have true feelings for.

When the man of her "dreams" came along, she wasn't available. But she made herself available to him. I am not sure exactly what happened; I can only imagine. Either she found out that the man of her dreams had some bad habits, or the one she cheated on decided he didn't want to be with a woman who considered him second best. Maybe, just maybe, she decided that she didn't want to settle. The latter possibility is the ending I am going to imagine; it makes me feel hopeful.

I have been married to the same man for more than seventeen years, and having sex with him for even longer. I am not shy in the least, but I am not interested in sharing myself with another man. My husband knows "every inch" of my body, whether he wants to know it or not. I could not imagine sharing with another man what I have shared with my husband for the past eighteen years—my mind, body and spirit. Even when things are not going well between the two of us, I don't want to contaminate what we have by straying away and introducing something that could devastate my husband if he were to find out. Furthermore, I am fully aware of the possible consequences of doing such a thing, which could be equally devastating to both of us.

What would you do if you found out that you have been

cheated on? Better yet, what would you do if a friend broke the news to you? Would that friend become your enemy or would you accept the news as the gospel?

When I found out that I was in the process of being replaced with another woman, I was angry with the messenger. The messenger was a friend. My anger may have been somewhat misdirected, but she was not completely right. She was not right because of what I perceived her intentions were. The night before she spilled the beans to me, she ran into my then boyfriend. He was the same guy that I have mentioned earlier—the one that had broken someone else's heart by replacing her with me. My friend said that she had seen him in the club with another couple, all hugged up with another woman. She remarked that when he saw her, he made no attempt to adjust himself, as if he was daring her to say something. She let me know that she didn't like his perceived arrogance.

I felt let down by her because she broke the news to me with an impersonal phone call. I was a friend. At the very least, I deserved the courtesy of her delivering that kind of news in person. I was in love with him. I had hoped that I would spend the rest of my life with him. (Thank God I didn't!) She should have taken the time to be there for me, in person, to help with my grieving process. But I felt that she was trying to beat him to the punch—engaging in some sort of twisted challenge with him—to give her view of what happened before he could. I'm not sure if she was concerned about how it was going to affect me. The only easing into the conversation that was made was her asking me if I had seen or talked with him that day. But to her credit, I don't believe that her intention was to hurt me, even though she did.

Ultimately, I was angry with myself; I already knew about him. I didn't have to investigate whether the news she had imparted to me was true. The only thing she did was to gain knowledge of something that had been privately known for weeks. I was also angry because I was forced to make a decision about him before I was ready to do so. It was one thing for me to be a fool when no one else was looking. I could not allow myself to be *observed* as one.

Communication

8

It could never be emphasized enough that communication is one of the keys necessary in order to have a successful relationship. If I were a man who has come home to an angry woman ranting and raving, neck gyrating, with one hand on the hip, and the other hand's pointer finger pointing at me, I wouldn't want to respond to *that* myself. I don't believe that everything I think or feel should be said in the heat of the moment. I rather believe in dealing with issues immediately when they arise. I would attempt to put the person I am trying to communicate with, in the moment, into the picture of what is about to happen and try and get them to see their accountability for their actions. I would do it so they could see how I feel about what has been done to me without acting like a victim. Ultimately, I also have to understand my part in the situation.

I remember distinctly when I was having some issues with my husband early on in our marriage. I was speaking openly to a friend about what I was going through with him and her response was, "You know how men are!" I felt that my feelings were dismissed and she went on to talk about the incompetence of men and their shortcomings. What I got from the conversation, in that very moment, was that she was not effectively communicating with me.

I wanted to talk; she didn't want to hear it. And what I got from the conversation was that it didn't matter what I was going through. I was to let him be, and allow my expectations of him to be non-existent, or of no consequence, and move on. But how do you move on when there is no resolution? You can't! You get stuck in emptiness, because there is a void. You then become just like every other unhappy person out there. That is not what I wanted for myself. I wanted to be happy. Thank goodness, I thought for myself and ignored everything she said to me. In doing so, I have become an effective communicator. In turn, I have a decent relationship with my husband, and we are raising our children together; we are continuing to learn how to communicate with one another.

Not communicating effectively is a major reason why many relationships fail. The reason is because the people involved in the relationship are trying to be "right." And it's not about who is right, it's about trying to get "it" right. In the beginning of our marriage, my husband was very selfish, and it was *always* all about him. And let me just say it now, no matter how well you think you know a person, you don't really start to learn who they are until you're married to them (i.e. cohabiting), and that is part of the problem.

A major reason why many people are not able to effectively communicate is because there is a miscommunication of what is expected. It would seem natural that if your partner knows what is expected of them, they would be able to give you what you need. Many of us become involved in relationships and marriage without truly knowing who our partner is—such as their financial status, political preference, or whether they want to have children, etc. And the reason people are not making their expectations known is out of fear that it will lead to rejection, or to having an answer which they are not willing to face.

Early in my marriage to my husband, I tried to be a good wife by cooking him a decent meal whenever I was off from work. It wasn't long before I noticed that I was cooking for myself. He would disregard my meal and go out and buy himself something from a fast-food joint, without asking me if I wanted anything. I was not happy about it and told him so. His response was that what I prepared was not what *he* wanted to eat. I told him that it was okay that he didn't want to eat what I had cooked, but I felt that he didn't appreciate my effort, and he was wasting *our* money.

It seemed absurd to me that a grown man could walk into a kitchen and see a countertop and stove filled with prepared food and not think it was important to say to me that he didn't want it. Or how he could see me prepare food and not comment on it if it was something he didn't like. Perhaps I could have asked him what he would have liked to eat. Did he think I was preparing it all for myself? What the hell did he think it was for? Simply a dish I prepared for him to look at? Not only that, like I said, when he went out to buy food, he wouldn't even ask *me* if I wanted anything. Damn!

Thank God he didn't have any food allergies; if he had any, I wouldn't have known. It became clear to me that we didn't know as much as we should have known about one another. It may seem ridiculous that I am using a food analogy for effective communication, but the goal here is to stress that from that point on, I became aware that we didn't know enough about each other's preferences, and not just where food was concerned. I also didn't know that I had married a man who would have completely disregarded my efforts. We should have been aware of those and other things about one another before saying "I Do." The good thing with that situation is that he apologized for it and we started to plan our meals together. We also agreed that we would be in accord with each other about this, and other decisions, that required both of our participation.

When you become disappointed in your man, instead of him coming home to an angry woman, let him come home to a woman who is willing to sit down with him to discuss what is happening in the relationship to cause you aggravation or despair. Avoid a confrontation; a confrontation's intention is to put someone on the spot. That person will no longer be able to hear a word you are saying because they will immediately become defensive. Instead of having a confrontation, think of it as having a conversation, without anger if possible, and from a place of compassion; compassion not for him, but for yourself, because of your need to be heard. Without it, nothing will be accomplished from the both of you being angry, which usually results in a lot of yelling, a headache, and sore throat.

For many years after being married, whenever I'd try to communicate with my husband about an issue, he'd take it personally, whether it was about him or not. And Lord have mercy, if I was indeed speaking of something *personal* about him that troubled me, or that I felt he did wrong, he would verbally attack me as though I wanted to make him feel bad about *himself!* When I realized that it was what he thought—he admitted this—I would look him in the eyes in a way that his only choice was to look back into mine, and ask him, "Is that what you really think of me? Is that the kind of woman you think you married?"

When he realized that he was wrong, he tried to use word games to win the arguments, but I wouldn't let him, and I still don't. When people use word games to win arguments, it is only because they are fearful of being found out. Fearful of others finding out they don't know jack, that they are insecure and unsure of themselves, or because they are afraid to be found out as a fraud.

Communicating with my husband has not always been easy. Many times when I thought I was being clear about what I was saying to him, he would be all wrong in his perception and therefore took it as a verbal attack on him. When that happened, he would become someone that I couldn't recognize, and therefore someone who wasn't hearing me. Yes, it's true; it's not what you do, but how you do it. But no matter what or how I said something, he would still misinterpret it; he wanted to be angry. He wasn't trying to understand. The word games would start when he couldn't win the argument, and that's when the disconnection would happen.

I often think back to the days when things were not the best between the two of us. If it had been bad enough that divorce would have been considered as an option, I imagined how he could have become mean and nasty and attempt to fight for custody of my children, just to stick it to me. Because when he misunderstood my intentions, or couldn't win an argument with me, I literally could see the change in him by the look in his eyes; he morphed into someone else, not the same man I had married. He wasn't the man I laughed with, laughed at, or the one who said he loved me. He was completely disconnected from me. But that was *his* choice, not mine, because I would try *hard* to reach him with my words. *He* had to finally be the one to realize that he wanted to be touched by what I had to say so that we could be on the same page. He also had to do it so that we could try and fix what was wrong between the two of us, rather than making the argument about he said, she said, or who's right vs. who's wrong.

His being mean and nasty was his way of trying to control the situation, or me, but I would never "submit" to it, and that was the frustrating part for him. Frustrating because he had never had to work so hard, or at all, to maintain a relationship between himself and a woman. For most men in relationships, it is easy when they are not the ones having to make all of the sacrifices; it's a no-brainer. With most men, all they have to do to be a part of a relationship is to "breathe," and the woman is the one who makes everything else happen. But a real relationship, especially of the married kind, is not that easy.

I will admit, I don't make things easy for my husband, and on occasion, I have been known to give him plenty of hell. Maybe that was my way of trying to control him. I needed more from him than he was giving, and I wouldn't submit; I couldn't! It would have meant that I was giving up on what I wanted so that he could be satisfied. I am grateful, though, that I didn't marry a man with anger-management issues. Had he been the short-tempered, violent-type, he would have wanted to slap the shit out of me for aggravating him. But what he is, is the type of man that is willing to put up with me, as I am willing to put up with him, because we ultimately want the same things: to be in a loving, two-parent home raising our children.

Communicating effectively is essential in order to get to the bottom of things so accountability can be assigned; it takes two to tango. Playing word games ultimately boils down to not being serious about getting to the bottom of what is causing the ailment in the relationship. Over time, my husband eventually confessed to me that he responded to me thusly out of feelings of insecurity, and because it was the only way he knew how to retaliate. I am not "*his*" enemy, and he knows that now. My intention is never to hurt his person, in any way. He is my husband, and if he is successful, then so am I.

Trust and Honesty

9

Another key to a successful relationship is to have trust and the ability to be honest, although not necessarily at all costs. It is one thing to be honest, but to hurt someone's feelings needlessly is unnecessary. Communication and honesty go hand in hand, and trust goes hand in hand with honesty. There can be no trust without honesty and no honesty without trust.

Many people think that trusting someone has something to do with the other person, but it doesn't. You have to trust yourself in order to trust others. If people have proved themselves to be untrustworthy and they continue to participate in your life, then you should *not* trust them. Let's use a backstabbing co-worker as an example. You would not trust them, but you'd continue to work alongside them being ever pleasant. However, you probably wouldn't put up pretenses to sit and have lunch with them after finding out about their evil ways.

On the other hand, by allowing the untrustworthy person to continue to have a major part in your life, you have chosen to give over to them your ability to trust them. An example for this is marrying the man who cheated on you, or treated you horribly. How can you trust that person again? I don't know, but it would be my opinion that it is difficult without some clear understanding as to why it happened. I'm not suggesting the obvious thing to do; to leave that person, although, of course, it is an option. What I am suggesting is that at the point of distrust, there should be some level of honesty you have to be willing to establish between yourself and that person. Otherwise, you will be giving away your ability to trust them, to them.

In a nutshell, when people do something to prove themselves as untrustworthy, don't turn a blind eye to it. Be honest with yourself by accepting what has happened. Deal with it first by acknowledging what happened and your role in it. If it was no fault of your own, then you know the ownership of it belongs to that person who has wronged you.

If your man has cheated on you before, then what's to stop him from doing it again, if this issue has never been dealt with to its core? I mean, come on, if every time he goes out and you question his every move, where he is going, who he's going with, and what time he'll be back, there's something wrong. And when he returns home, the interrogation starts all over again.

What is all of that about; him or you? Him, because he did something that was wrong, or you, because you think it's about trusting him? If you had dealt with it in the beginning, all of that wouldn't be necessary. And because it has not been dealt with, the distrust will never end. Wouldn't you like to have an end to the distrust? You can do so by trusting yourself, first and foremost. Trust what you see. Trust what you know. Above all else, trust what you *feel!* Trust your intuition by trusting yourself so that you can get to a place where you no longer believe that trusting others has to do with them, but has everything to do with you.

Insecurity comes from not trusting yourself. That is probably why many men don't feel free in the relationship they have with their women. Not only is he interrogated before he leaves the house, but once he returns, the interrogation goes to another level. I have heard many tales of men going out for the evening and when he gets home, his woman wants to know every detail of his evening out without her, including sniffing him to see if she can smell the scent of another woman.

My husband once went out for the evening and the first thing he did when he came home, after saying hello and that he had a good time, was get into the shower. Because I had brought some of my baggage from an old relationship into this one, he was caught off-guard. I asked him why he had to jump straight into the shower; he had taken one before he left to go out. He said, "Because I smell like smoke. I sat there in that bar all night while people were smoking and I don't want it on me!"

His response was simple enough, and I had no other basis for not trusting him. So I had to learn to trust myself by letting him be, and deal with whatever as it came. It was a lesson for me. My husband has given me no reason not to trust him with my person, although my past experiences had taught me to not trust others and myself. You can't blindly go through life by trusting everyone. But you also can't go around thinking it's everyone's intention to pull the wool over your eyes. It is not about believing what he says; it's about believing what he does, and what I feel. It is about trusting yourself to do the right thing when you know that you have been wronged. Because as you know, when it quacks like a duck... Ultimately, it is all about seeing that big-ass pink elephant in the room that no one wants to talk about.

Now let's be honest! Honestly..."honesty" is a very scary word for some. It seems that some people equate honesty with heartbreak or with the feeling of impending doom. How would you feel when someone says to you, "We need to talk... let me just be honest?" These are very ominous statements; especially when you don't know what is to follow. Stop living in fear of what is to come; what will be will be. You can't change the inevitability of what is going to happen, but you can prepare yourself by understanding people's intentions.

It would be difficult for me to talk about trust and honesty without talking about the word *intention*. Intention is a mighty powerful, influential word. If you know a person's intention from the get-go, then you will have a better understanding of what is to come. Some men's primary intention is just to hit it and be gone; while you're over here crying your eyes out, he's over there going on with his life. He doesn't know your pain; only his pleasure. If you weren't so blind in the beginning to see it for what it was, rather than what you wanted it to be, you could have seen his intentions a mile away. How can I be so sure? Because everything is supposed to make sense, and when it doesn't, you should smell the stench of a lying dog. If it quacks like a duck...

Way before my husband and I got together, I once dated a married man (unbeknownst to me). He said that his sister was living with him and I believed his assertion because I wanted to. I should've known better when he never invited me to his home, or by the fact that I didn't know his home phone number. He called me; I didn't call him. Another time, I dated a guy who would never leave my apartment. I come to find out that he was essentially homeless. If a guy only wants to hang out with you and no one else, he could probably be trying to isolate you from your other friends or family. You may think it's cute that he only wants to be with you, but it's not. He may have something to hide. No one person should be the center of another's universe; it's unnatural, unhealthy and dysfunctional.

Getting back to intention and its power: *Everything* said and done has an intention. It's not just what is said or done, it's how it is said or done. If I had on a pair of high-heeled boots and someone said to me, "I don't like those boots!" What is the point of that statement? Clearly, it would be to make me feel insecure (good thing for me is that I don't look to other people for validation or acceptance). My response would simply be, "Good thing you don't have to wear them!" My intention with my response would be to let that person know that I don't need their opinion of my boots or me. It is possible, however, that the person only meant to point out that they could not wear boots with such high heels. But because that was not what was said, I would have to assume their intention was to create chaos.

So if a man says he loves you, wants to marry you, or wants to be the father of your children after only knowing you for a very short time, are you to assume that he means it, or does he have an ulterior motive? I don't know, but I would be more inclined to believe the latter. Why? Because love is a verb, it's the act of doing; it's not something that's said, it's something that's done. If a man wants all of the aforementioned from you, then it would have to be his intention to prove it to you. If he can't prove it, then his intentions were less than honorable and it is your responsibility to know the difference!

Although I went on a tangent for a moment with regard to intention, I want to get back on target and talk about honesty again. I was saying how much I believe in being honest (and not necessarily at all costs). My husband, for one, may disagree as to the cost. He thinks that sometimes I say too much. I don't agree. But I have taken his opinion into consideration.

In the past, when he'd buy me a gift, which was not of my liking, I would tell him so. He would be furious! I couldn't understand his anger; especially when my tone was neither judgmental nor hostile. I didn't think I was being mean, but if he asked me how I liked it, I would be honest. He thought I should have just been *grateful*, and I was, that he thought enough of me as to not forget a special day like my birthday, or an anniversary.

Well, I don't want to treat my husband like I would my children. If my children bought me a gift from the discount store, I would act like it was the best thing since sliced bread! However, I don't want my husband to have this false sense of who or what I am, just so that he can feel good about the gift he's given me. I don't want my husband to spend our money on something I would or could never have any use for. I don't want to treat my husband the way that I would treat my children by pretending that his gift was the best ever. I would rather my husband really know who I am and what my tastes in things are.

If I hadn't been honest with him, then he'd still be thinking he knows me better than anyone else, which wouldn't be true, and this despite the fact that I sleep next to him every night. We'll share with a girlfriend about a useless or terrible gift our man gave us, but we'll make him think it was the best thing ever, that he did a good thing by remembering the date. But guess what? That's his job, to remember. Now I don't know about you, but if I gave my man a gift and he didn't like it, I'd rather he tell me so that I can know his likes and dislikes. It goes back to that word "intention" again. My intention was not to call attention to how wrong his gift was for me, but for him to understand what kind of woman he is married to. It makes no sense to me that we claim to know one another so well, but have no earthly idea about what each other's likes or dislikes are.

Speaking of trust and honesty (and perhaps infidelity), when I was in nursing school, I met a doctor, an intern. He was young, gifted (if you know what I mean) and Black. He was married, although I didn't much concern myself with it because I wasn't trying to marry him (I was young and immature.) When he took my phone number, he wrote it down like he was taking a medical history. If my phone number, for example, was 555-2035, he wrote it down in medical terminology that would read as: fifty-year-old Black female with children ranging in age from twenty to thirty-five years. He was slick. That little trick kept him from getting in trouble if his wife were to ever discover it.

We talked frequently and had phone sex. He even invited me over to his townhouse that he shared with his children and wife. I was so stupid! I went over and all he did was tease me. I should have never been there, but I was. It was stupid and immature of me to let myself get caught up in nothing.

Physical sex never happened between the two of us; only heavy petting and kissing. We continued to have phone sex with each other because we obviously had nothing else better to do. I remember seeing him in the movie theater with his wife. They were there seeing the same movie that my mother and I had just seen— *Malcolm X.* When he noticed me, he winked at me. I suppose it was to make me feel special; it didn't. I remember thinking to myself that I would hate to end up married to a man who would treat me in such a disrespectful way, coming on to another woman in my presence. Back then I thought that being cheated on was a way of life. I didn't think that the disrespectful part was being cheated on, because I thought the saying was true: "What you don't know won't hurt you!"

Not too long after that, on a Sunday afternoon, he called me. He told me that he confessed to his wife that he almost had sex with another woman. I was in shock and not really sure how to take what he was saying. Somehow she ended up on the phone talking to me. I was *really* shocked by now! After I got over my shock, I became pissed at him for putting me in the middle of the game he was playing with his wife.

I knew what his intentions were. I may have been stupid (young and immature) back then, but I wasn't clueless. Either she had discovered it on her own and he had no other choice, or he came out with it on his own to play his wife (and me) to make her feel insecure and jealous. It's possible that he wanted to test his worth by seeing if we were going to get into a duel over him. Hardly!

I imagined that after his apologies to her for his bad behavior, he had make-up sex with her while professing his undying love for her. I also imagined that during the process of his making up to her, she was overwhelmed with emotion because she felt grateful that he loved her enough to "tell her the truth," or because of her enduring love for him, or because he chose her over someone else!

If it seems as though my words are sarcastic, it is because they *are!* Not to poke fun at her, but rather because I know men like him; the ones who play games, and then turn it around on the woman as though it's her that is insecure. You know, playing word games. But the one that was really insecure was him; I can see no other point to doing what he did except to play a game so that she could show him how much she loved him and how much she was willing to endure for the love of him.

I heard such sadness in her voice, not pissed-off ness, as she should have been. However, as sad as she may have been, she tried to go off on me! While on the phone with me, she asked me how I could do something like that. In the same breath, she asked me if I knew that he was married. I told her that it was not important that *I* knew he was married; what was important was that *he* remembered he was married!

Although we didn't have sex with one another, he cheated on her emotionally. He allowed himself to have a personal connection/relationship with another woman. He also allowed another woman to come into the home that he shared with his family. And for his wife's sake, it is a good thing that I was mentally stable since I knew more about her than she knew about me. Imagine how I could have taken advantage of the situation if I were different and wanted more from him than what he was willing to give; it could have been a fatal attraction. Then for sure it would have been, "What you don't know, can hurt you!"

It would be difficult, again, to talk about trust and honesty, without talking about truthfulness. I started this book off by talking about some of the things that I don't understand. One thing I didn't mention, which is a pet peeve of mine, is **LYING** unnecessarily, and being lied to. I could also add I hate being lied about, and I do, but I have no control over that.

I know people who have lied on me for no apparent reason. But what can I do about it? I have to assume that there is something about me that they either want or don't have. The purpose, therefore, would be to make me look bad in someone else's eyes, or make them feel good about themselves. But the only person responsible for making me look bad is me. If someone judges me based on what someone else says, shame on them. The only thing I can control is my reaction to it, or whether I will allow those people to have an important part in my life... not!

I dated a guy for about six months before I realized the name I had been calling him by was not his real name. Can you imagine how silly I felt when I realized I had been screwing someone that I didn't even know? For me, being lied to can be a deal breaker. Needless to say, it didn't last long afterward.

I would be lying if I said my husband never lied to me. He has. They were, for the most part, white, unnecessary and silly lies. Lying can be by omission. It can also be when someone pretends to be something they are not. My husband is definitely guilty of that. Because like I said, he is no longer the man that I dated. While we dated he pretended to be someone altogether different than what he is. I thought that he was so "together." I married him and found out that he was on his "best behavior" until he closed the deal. But whatever trust issues I may have had with him never had anything to do with whether he loved me or not, or whether I could trust him with my person. I have never doubted what I meant to him.

When we first got together, I didn't know that he had been married. Let me clarify. Before my husband and I got together, I heard that he was married. I got it from the horse's mouth that yes, he had been married, but at the time we got together, he had been divorced for one year. It wasn't until we were married that I found out that his divorce had been final for less than six months prior to our union. When I discovered this information, I called him out on it. He said that he didn't want me to think that he was on the rebound when we got together. Was he lying about that? Maybe, but this is the longest rebound relationship I have ever heard of.

When I was a little girl, I was accused of doing something that I didn't do. I can't even remember what it was, but I wasn't guilty of it! It made me feel awful inside. It happened because I was asked a question. I suppose that since my answer was not what the person wanted to hear, I was called a *liar*!

I have never forgotten what that felt like, being called a liar. Someone looking me dead in my face, and despite my telling the truth, as I knew it, I was labeled a liar! It changed something in me. I never wanted to feel like that again. It doesn't mean that I haven't told a white one. But to live a life where everything that is said from my mouth is an untruth is immature, dysfunctional and unacceptable.

Have you ever known a person with whom everything they say is suspect? Some people make up shit just to have something to say, and it makes no sense at all. Like India.Arie says in her song "The Truth:" "There ain't no substitute for the truth, either it is or isn't; you see, the truth it needs no proof, either it is or isn't!"

I could talk about women and our issues with trusting men for days, but what about a man being able to trust a woman who has shown herself to be untrustworthy? How many times have women lied about being pregnant to get a man to stay with them? How many times have women gotten intentionally pregnant to grab themselves a big payoff? How many women get pregnant and lie about whom the father of the baby is? This type of woman exists everywhere. After all of her lies, she still wants to have that man in her life and feel trust. But how can there be trust when the foundation of a relationship is based on lies?

Accountability

10

Stop it, stop it now, stop it right now! Stop blaming anything and everything for not having the life you think you deserve! How many of you say, "I'd be happy if only…"—which may translate to *if he'll marry me*, *if I lived in that house*, or *if I could just have a baby*, then *my life would feel complete*! This is an absolute and utter falsehood, to ever believe that your ultimate happiness depends on anything or anyone else but you.

I really could have summed up this book in one word: accountability. I believe it is the greatest gift that I have ever been taught, and it will be the greatest I can endeavor to teach to my children. It can't be given to someone; it has to be taught by example. I work in a colorful environment with a bouquet of different people that are grouped by their different personalities. One of the things that I have come to realize is that the work environment is not only akin to a soap opera; it is also a playground where people are divided into groups.

Grown folks on the job are separated much like kids are on the playground. Sometimes, starting on a new job is much like starting a new school. Every group of kids is sizing you up to decide if it's their group that will let you gain admission. You know the groups I'm talking about—the popular kids, the bullies, the rich kids, the smart kids, the nerds, etc. Many grown people have not been able to make a successful transition from childhood to adulthood. It seems in my experience that this is the case more often than not. It would be a great experience to behold if the majority of adults who pass through my life would be more adult-like than child-like in their ability to be accountable for their actions.

Years ago my husband and I participated in a garage sale in our subdivision—it was subdivision wide. We had neighbors, friends, who lived across the street that were involved as well. During that time, I spent most of my time in the house taking care of housework, while my husband hung outside with our neighbors. So whenever we got customers he would run back to our garage to conduct the sale. The last time he did so, he left our daughter (who was two at the time) at the neighbors' house (they had a three-year-old son who was present.) This time, after my husband finished with the sale, he came into the house. I was in the office downstairs and noticed that after he'd been in for a long minute or two, the door to my house from the garage opened and my baby came in saying, "Hey, Mama." I looked at her, waiting for an adult to walk in after her. It never happened!

I looked outside, expecting to see them showing an indication that they noticed she was missing. They didn't seem to notice that she was no longer there. I was a little disturbed by it, but more disturbed by what eventually transpired. The weekend passed and my heart could not allow me to be okay with what happened without speaking my mind. I thought that's what friends do; talk to one another to gain an understanding of the other's feeling or perspective. So come Monday evening I called and spoke to the wife and my words were "I love you, and I know beyond a shadow of a doubt that you didn't mean for it to happen, but I want to know what happened." I tried really hard not to seem confrontational.

I was first offended because she asked me what I was talking about which, to me, meant that she was either playing dumb, or my baby and her safety meant nothing to her. When I explained myself (which I should not have had to do), she said a whole bunch of nothing. By now, I was hearing her husband in the background ranting and raving. He was saying my child's name as though it was a derogatory word. He took the phone from his wife and continued his rant toward me. In his anger-induced litany, he referred to the fact that I had obviously upset his wife by asking questions I had a right to ask. I wanted to know exactly what had happened that day, and the fact that I never had anyone say "boo" to me about it. If I had to guess, they felt that since it was over, and no one was hurt, that all should have been good. He sounded incensed that I would have the nerve to question *anything*! He had some nerve, raising his voice at me, as though I didn't have a right as a friend, or as a mother, to express myself regarding what happened and what could have potentially happened. I politely excused myself from the phone, citing that I had things to do.

The only thing I had to do was to put my shoes on and go across the street to deal with the situation face to face. My husband was upset by now because he saw how troubled I was. However, I don't think, not even to this day, that he fully understands my angst. But even so, he got dressed and followed me because he was afraid of the outcome if he hadn't. Once I was there, they did everything they could to seem busy. I told them, I'd sit and wait until I could have their undivided attention. Once they stopped to talk with me, they tried to explain to me that what happened to my baby girl was "just one of those things." What does "one of those things" mean? I thought it meant something like having a bad day (for no apparent reason), or being in a traffic jam. How did my two-year-old baby crossing the street alone become "just one of those things"?

Without going into minute details, what eventually happened is that I said to the two of them, while looking directly into the woman's eyes, that someone had to be accountable for what happened. So since she (they) couldn't be, I would be. Their response to me was to say that I was not to blame for what happened. But there was something in the tone of her voice—it was not what she said, but definitely how she said it. She said it as though she wanted to alleviate me of the guilt of my child walking across the street alone. She was serious! What upset me the most about the conversation was that she treated what happened, truly, just like "one of those things." And to think that I had, in the not so distant past, seen her literally hold her son's wrist so tightly to keep him safe from being hit by the cars in the street, that if her grasp were any tighter he would have lost all feeling in it. She refused to see the severity of what had happened, or the possibility of what could have happened to my baby and what ultimately was at stake: our friendship.

The conversation ended with my assuming responsibility for what had happened. I needed to. Someone had to be responsible for what happened, or what could have happened to my baby. I took responsibility of it because, if I hadn't allowed her to be left there, it wouldn't have happened. I left her with friends who I thought would value her, as they would their own child. But instead, what I realized was that they didn't take my friendship seriously enough to understand that it was important that they have some dialogue with me regarding what happened. They wanted to sweep it under the rug and allow us all to go on with our lives, the way it was before that day. It was a very stressful time in my life; I lived across the street from these people, who I had thought were my friends. They couldn't even value me enough, as a friend or mother, to just say, "I'm sorry that your baby walked across the street alone."

I believe they felt bad about what happened, but how they handled it damaged the possibility of my having anything more to do with them than just having friendly conversation. They are no different from other people who want to put blinders on and hope that a situation goes away. But that's not how life goes, if you don't deal with things as they happen and you get bit in the ass, you'll have no one else to blame but yourself. If I had allowed myself to continue as friends with them, because I no longer trusted them, something else would have happened for them to disappoint me. I would have had no one else to blame but myself, because they had already shown me that they were incapable of being the kind of friends that I needed them to be.

It was easier for them to say it was nobody's fault because it absolved them of any wrongdoing or guilt. But guess what? It's okay to be wrong or make mistakes and you are a bigger person for being able to say so. If they had been willing to talk about the situation from a bigger perspective than blame or to take their foolish pride out of the equation, we would still be friends today.

Sex

11

How can I write this book without talking about what used to be one of my favorite things to do, besides shop?! I say *used to* because while my husband and I have a healthy sexual relationship, children, work, household duties and life have gotten in the way of us being able to perform like rabbits! Sex has been a part of my life since I started having it; I love it! I have been having it for more than twenty-eight years, and I have been having a ball! I must say though, when done just right, this is a reason, besides being treated well by a man, for which I could have lost my mind over a man. He could have all my money!

I had been having sex for many years until I had my world rocked. The guy I talked about earlier, the one that broke my heart, was an *unbelievable* lover. Every time I would see him, my stomach would do flips. Ooo wee, when I'd see him, I couldn't wait to be alone with him because I knew what was coming. It was one of the biggest reasons why I hated to break up with him; who else was going to give me loving like he did? As time went on, I learned that there were other fish in the sea and they were just as good, if not better. I also learned that if they were not as good, they could become great because my experience taught me how to tutor them.

I learned many things about men like him. I learned that being a great lover was all he had to offer; he knew he wasn't in the relationship with me for the long haul. He also wanted to make the experience stimulating and exciting for me so that I would long for him. Because if I longed for him, I would allow him to be in my life, even if that meant that I would have to share him with someone else. However, my sexual experience with him taught me a lot about what I wanted from sex. It also taught me a lot about myself. He introduced me to a few new things (you'll have to use your imagination) and once the relationship was over, I continued using those new things for my own benefit.

The relationship with my "lover boy" (this is the name I will refer to him as for the rest of this book) may have been over, but I was able to take the experience to become a better lover, not just for myself but also for the partner that I chose. Even though he left me broken-hearted, I learned things about myself sexually. What I wanted and didn't want. How I wanted it and didn't want it.

I can't speak on the subject of sex without talking about sexual responsibility. I used contraceptives effectively and was able to avoid an unplanned pregnancy. Even though I was on the pill, however, there were a few times when I didn't use a condom. *HOW STUPID!* I thought you could tell that a guy was clean by looking at him. I ignored the fact that it is not just pregnancy or regular STDs you have to concern yourself with; there is also HIV. Those other STDs are tame in comparison to HIV. Even though it is not necessarily a death sentence, I have seen a few people lose their battle with the disease. You simply cannot afford in the year 2011 to have the same ignorant, immature thoughts about sexual behavior. If you are dating a man who refuses to have sex with you because he doesn't want to use a condom, then don't fuck him. Tell him that if he wants to get fucked real good, it can only be done with a condom on!

Being sexually responsible is about your being responsible for your own sex life in how you experience it. If you're sexually active, you should be enjoying yourself; if not, why aren't you? Don't allow yourself to be used by a man for your body. I can remember a time of sexual immaturity: I would be with a guy and the only thing he thought foreplay was for was to get my body ready to receive him! Yuck! You know what I mean. He'd lick his finger and tickle this and tickle that, and once I was moist, the foreplay was over and within two minutes, so was the rest!

Well, that would never last for very long. I would try and ease him into something different. If he couldn't catch on to my subtleties, I would be honest with him so I could bring him up to speed. Some men don't take kindly, I have heard, to being told "how to do it." But I can't be worried about how he will feel about something that also involves me, considering the fact that I would not be enjoying myself as much as him. It makes no sense that I would fake an orgasm so that his ego can be spared.

If he continues to make himself unavailable to me during the act of sex, to fail to realize that I was a part of the process, then shit on him! I don't want a man looking at me as if the only thing I am for him is a reservoir; he can go to the sex shop for that kind of thing. I was not going to accept that kind of behavior. Not from a man who I would have chosen to be a part of something that is extraordinary, my *Honey Pot*!!

How you experience your sex life is up to you. You should never allow your body to be used for someone else's pleasure. If you're not getting anything out of the process, or you're being hurt in the process, what is the point? I had been having sex for years before I knew what an orgasm was, and oh my goodness, once I found out, I became a changed woman.

There are many different forms of sexual activity ranging from oral to anal sex. To some they are abhorrent. I say to each his own. If you are going to engage in an alternate form of sex, please, please let it be because it's what *you* want. If you let it be about what the other person wants, you're allowing yourself to be used and to be seen only as a sex object. Also, never, ever use sex as a weapon or toy; you could find yourself in a situation not of your own choosing, even though no means no!

My mother spoke openly and clearly about sex with all of her children from a very early age. I was ten years old when I got my period. That was way too soon, but because I had older sisters in the home, I wasn't caught off-guard. It was something that was spoken often about in our home. I learned that my body was capable of having babies, and that I was too young to have sex.

My mother grew up in a home where there was not much talk about boys, men, babies, menstrual cycles, etc. As a result of not having what she needed, she ended up being pregnant at the age of thirteen by an adult man, and becoming a mother at the very tender age of fourteen. I admired the fact that even though she was a very young mother, she was a mother no less. My mother's honesty with her children was because she didn't want what happened to her to happen to us.

It is nothing new that the old school of teaching girls about sex is that you didn't talk about it. It was either never talked about, or girls were told many falsehoods about sex and where babies come from. One friend said that she was told that you get pregnant when a boy just touches you! Needless to say, she was devastated when a boy fell on top of her on the playground in school. She says she was almost inconsolable.

She was taken to the counselor's office and was asked by the counselor why she thought she was pregnant. She told the counselor what happened: "A boy touched me!" The counselor informed her that it is not how you get pregnant, but she didn't believe it!

She still didn't believe it when her older sister, who was a bit more experienced than she was, told her the same thing. I guess she finally realized it was true many months later when her body didn't go through any changes, because she wouldn't have dared ask her mother.

Back in the day, kids would get a spanking for talking about someone being pregnant. Another friend said that she was told that babies come out of the dark vertical line (linea nigra) that pregnant women get on their belly. I have even heard someone else say that when she first got her period, she never had a discussion with her mother about it then or ever. These stories may sound outrageous, but they are real.

I was allowed to date when I was sixteen years old. My mother always said to me that when I felt as though I was ready for sex, I needed to let her know. Well, my boyfriend tried to convince me that I was ready. I told my mother that I felt I was ready for sex, and she said to me, "No, you are not!" Fortunately I was more concerned with her being disappointed with me for doing something that she would disapprove of, rather than his being angry with me for not giving him what he wanted. Our relationship, slowly but surely, changed until it ended. He started dating another girl, I assumed, because he thought she would give him what he wanted a bit more easily.

The year that I would turn nineteen, I started dating a guy who was a few years older than me. He was twenty-two. Very shortly after that, my mother had a heart-to-heart with me about sex. Again, she talked about the fact that sex was not a bad thing. She told me that what makes it acceptable is when the two consenting people involved in it are doing it of their own free will, and that no one in the process would be hurt. She knew that there would be a time when the conversation of sex would come up during my new relationship, and I would have to be prepared for it and accept my choice to be with him or not.

I'll never, ever forget it. It was a Saturday evening when I returned home after being gone with him all day. My mother was in her bed reading a book, as she often does. Just as I walked into the house, she looked up from the book and looked over at me, over her glasses, and said to me, "Come here." I let out a big sigh, and walked over to her. She continued to look at me over her reading glasses and asked me if I had had sex. I was sooooo embarrassed. Not because I had something to hide, but because it was too soon afterward for me to feel comfortable in discussing it with her. I said straightforwardly that I had, so she asked me a barrage of questions, "Did he hurt you?", "How do you feel about it?", and "Are you okay?" I quickly answered her questions and she allowed me to leave the room.

I wasn't in love with the guy I lost my virginity to. I liked him, but I didn't love him the way you're supposed to love your "first." I don't mean to sound blasé about my first sexual experience, because it wasn't something I took lightly. I wanted to be with him because I loved him and enjoyed being with him. Not being head over heels for him is probably the thing that allowed me to move past him when things didn't work out. I remember my mother saying to me long before the loss of my virginity that she hoped my first time was with someone that I wasn't crazy in love with. She went on to explain that this was because she didn't want me to be devastated from the possible breakup and therefore make a terrible decision in an effort to keep him in my life.

Subconsciously I remember her saying that, but that is not the reason we didn't last. We didn't last because of him. I was only eighteen and he was twenty-two and he thought he knew more; he tried to mold me, especially after I lost my virginity to him.

He tried to use my inexperience as a way of controlling me. But thank goodness, I had already established a sense of myself long before he had come along. If he didn't realize it when we started dating, he realized it before we broke up; that I loved myself more than I could ever love him!

Sex is something that, when done just right, can be just like a drug. But you can't miss something you never had. If you are a virgin, it is something to be celebrated. It takes a lot of chutzpa to lead a life with satisfaction and freedom in spite of how others judge you, especially now, because we live in the time of "anything goes." Don't start something you are not able to finish. If you are engaging in sexual activity, be *responsible*! You owe it to yourself and to the people who depend on you.

Real Love

12

What is love exactly? One thing I've come to understand is that love can have a different meaning for different people. Another thing I understand is that most people don't know the meaning of it. How many times have you heard that love hurts? But is it love that actually hurts, or the loss of it? I think that it's the loss of it. If you have ever been left broken-hearted, ask yourself some serious questions about that person that you loved. Or, if they loved me, would they have hurt me so badly?

When people become purposeful in their quest to cause pain, that's not love. Are they trying to see how much you love them by putting you in the position to prove how much you love them? You have to love yourself more to know what love is when you see it. The problem is that most people are always looking for love outside of themselves, but in the end, they can't even recognize it when they see it!

It was shortly after college that I became involved with Lover Boy. I thought he was the bomb. He was Mr. Wonderful, in the beginning. He got me hooked on him and then took himself out of my equation. It was like going through some feeling not unlike withdrawal symptoms. I understand now that it was his intention all along, but I couldn't see it then. The truth is most men don't like being alone. With this knowledge, it's easy to understand why it was that he did not break it off with me, or the young lady before me, plainly and clearly.

When the dynamics of the relationship started to change, and he said nothing was wrong, I allowed myself to be satisfied with the response because he had said so. I wanted to believe what I heard and not what I *felt*. If he had told me that he was seeing someone else, he knew that there was a great possibility that I would have not continued the relationship, and when he found out that the grass wasn't greener on the other side, he would have been all alone.

What many men do, which is the same as what he did, is become moody and distant, including presenting a lack of intimacy. They become successful in making you feel insecure about the relationship despite their saying there is nothing wrong when asked. They begin to lay the foundation for their plan, preparing you for a potential change in the relationship. You'll just think that he is going through a "life" crisis. That's how you'll explain it to yourself. But his distance and moodiness is because he has been intimate, and not so distant, with someone or something else, and he doesn't want you to see or smell it on him. Then what happens is, either things will go back to normal because he found out the grass wasn't greener on that other front, or he decides to move on to what he assumes is greener pastures.

Even though I went through changes with Lover Boy I do believe that he did care for me, even loved me (by his definition of love), because we shared things that people in love share. However, his definition of love was not mine because if he loved me the way that I wanted to be loved, he would have not been apathetic about my pain. I am grateful, however, for the experience. Without it, who knows what I would have done to sacrifice myself (or my body) to keep him, then where would I be now?

As I have said before, *love* is a verb. Even in elementary school we are taught that a verb describes the act of something, like

raining, exercising, loving…you get my point. Most of us understand that, but for some reason, when it comes to love, we allow
ourselves to view it as something that's said, not acted on. If a
man whips your ass up and down the street but says he loves you,
which are you going to believe? What he says or what he does? If
your man's been gone away from home for days at a time and
says, still in a loving and reassuring voice, that he loves you and
he's not cheating, what are you going to believe—what he says or
what he does? When I eventually found out that I was sharing
Lover Boy with some other girl, a new one, I was devastated. I
still continued to see him, because I *loved* him (by my then definition). I remember he called me one night, and I was so *pleased*.
He said that he wanted to see me, but he didn't want to talk about
it (meaning her), and I replied sweetly and quietly, "okay." I just
wanted to be in his presence. I never thought that I was desperate
for a man, or would ever be willing to do what was necessary to
keep or get one, but I thought I was in love. He came over that
night and I did everything I could to keep him from leaving.
Because I knew that if he left he would be going to see her, and I
could not have that! I wanted to be the one who won. So for that
night I did win, but only for that one night.

The relationship got worse and I was eventually able to let go.
I am a firm believer, and I learned this from my mom, that you
don't have to break up with a person to get over them. Sometimes
staying with them allows you to start seeing them as they are. It's
like hanging on (to the relationship) with a rope that starts to
unravel. After a while, the rope becomes thin as thread, and it
breaks. And if you're smart you'll allow yourself time to experience
the breakup by learning more about yourself so as to not repeat
the situation.

What caused me to get over the relationship was asking myself some hard questions about the relationship. I loved him, but I loved the person that I thought he was, not what he had become (or should I say, what he revealed himself to be). I also asked myself why I was so bent out of shape about a guy with whom I hadn't invested that much time. It wasn't like we'd been going out for years; it was just shy of one year. You'd have thought that he was the last man on earth the way I went on and on with my grief. But what I did love about him was his generosity, his good lovemaking and his ability to make me feel like I was the only woman on earth for him. The problem was, I wasn't the only one he made feel that way!

There was no question that after that experience I had changed. My relationships with men also changed. That was a good thing. Even though he hurt me badly, I was able to rise up from the experience to learn many things about myself—about what I would or would not be willing to put up with, in *any* relationship, just to have one. Another thing I learned was that no matter how smart I thought I was (in dealing with men), I was not as educated as I believed myself to be in the ways of men.

I remember once when he gave me his new beeper number and he went out of town (supposedly) for the weekend with some friends. I tried repeatedly to get in touch with him, without success. I was finally able to talk with him once he got home. Now mind you, I was neither desperate for his affection nor jealous-minded, just in love. Up until that particular weekend, I had been in constant communication with him, so this was a new situation, not being able to get in touch with him. When I spoke with him, he apologized for giving me the incorrect beeper number—off by about two numbers. He says it was by mistake, although I doubt it. I thought nothing of it necessarily, except that I felt as though something in the water wasn't clean.

Without being invited to come over, I hopped into my car and went to his apartment. Before I left the house, my mother tried to discourage me from going unannounced. She feared that I would come across something I may not want to see. I told her that I wanted to know what was going on, whether good or bad. I got to his apartment and there was nothing to see. I left with a goodnight kiss and thought nothing else of it. I thought I had proven to myself that all was well, because remember, I thought I was smart enough to know better. Well, a few months following that day was when I found out I was sharing him with another woman. By then I was truly in love with him and unable to see how this could happen to me right under my eyes.

My mistake was being contented when I saw nothing that appeared suspicious during my visit to his apartment. It's not always what is staring you in the face; sometimes it is what you don't see. What man do you know who's been away from his woman for a few days, when he sees her, does nothing to keep her from leaving? Not only did he not ask me to come over, he let me leave and acted like he was tired from the trip. He kissed me goodnight and sent me on my merry way. I was satisfied to myself that I saw nothing, even though it was out of the ordinary. Because usually, when I'd go to visit him, I would stay the night. There was nothing wrong with him not wanting to be with me that night, but I didn't question (to myself) that it was out of the ordinary. It may seem like a small thing, but that's how these situations start.

Even though I thought I was smarter than any of my experiences prior to this one, I came out of it a more mature person. I was also able to truly see things as they were, and not as I wanted them to be. If I didn't know before, I knew then that I didn't want to be a person who didn't hear or see the big-ass elephant sitting in the room! So, whatever *it* is, I let it be. If it's ugly, it's ugly. If it's red, it's red. If it quacks like a duck…I promised myself that I would not be a person who would spray perfume on top of funk. If it is funky, it is funky. I will deal with the funk and move on!

Getting back to love, it is a magnificent thing! No matter how cliché this sounds, it's true. The only problem is, like I said earlier, people are unable to see it, even when they are surrounded by it. Too many of us women are looking for it outside of ourselves. We want desperately for someone to love us, while failing to realize that we *must* love ourselves first. I don't know how many times this statement has to be reiterated for *us* to get it! I can't tell you how to get to the point of loving yourself, except to say that if you don't, then, don't expect anyone else to be able to. I'm not trying to be funny, but how in the world can you expect anyone to love something you don't?

How many of you single mothers out there are desperate for love from a man? Of course, there's nothing wrong with wanting it, but being desperate for it is the problem. Because when you're desperate for something, it means you're willing to sacrifice yourself (or your beliefs) for it. For one thing, if you are a single mother, that in and of itself is a very hard job. Your priority is to your kids, no question. And if you're desperate for the love and affection of a man, then you've already decided that the love you get from your children is not enough.

I know firsthand because I am a mother, and I couldn't fathom someone else coming before my children. I strongly believe that if I were a single parent, that the love from my kids could sustain me. If it cannot in your situation, then Houston, you have a problem! Don't misunderstand me, because I don't want to seem insensitive or judgmental to the plight of single mothers. But if your need for love does not include the love from your children, then as I said earlier, you are not able to recognize love when you see it.

Don't get the need for love from a man confused with the need to have physical satisfaction. Neither has anything to do with the other. You can go to the sex shop for help to relieve that kind of tension. And forget about the excuses that I have heard from some women that, "I need someone to hold on to," because they think they're too "good" to use an artificial form of satisfaction.

What they really want to say is that they are embarrassed to talk about it, let alone have someone see them in a place like that purchasing something like that! Believe me when I say, they couldn't care less about your being there, because they are there for the same thing. Anyway, I guarantee it, what you'll get from that sex shop could be more powerful than anything you've ever experienced with a man. It'll do until the real thing, the right thing, comes along!

Single women without children also have the same problem, which is, focusing on the need for love from a man and being desperate for it. I don't get it! What's the hurry? Okay, maybe your biological clock is ticking, but including this, I can't understand why the desperation. You know as well as I do that a physical man is not needed to have children. As I said earlier, there's nothing wrong in wanting it, but being desperate for it is the problem. If you're desperate because of the need to have children, stop it now! Desperation causes you to ignore your intuition and therefore potentially puts you in the position of making what could be the worst mistake of your life. Having children is much more than a notion and therefore should not be taken lightly because of the desire to have them.

When Lover Boy and I broke up, I was distraught. I even wished that during the few times we were together after the breakup, I would get pregnant. *THANK YOU, GOD*, that I didn't! How many women have done that? Gotten pregnant from a man because of the desperation to keep him? Oftentimes the children are of no consequence to that man and he still moves on with his life. The children will then, for you, serve as a constant reminder of him and an obstacle to future suitors. Possibly then you will go around being pissed off at the world, thinking someone owes you something. You will be taking the anger out on your children and blaming them for everything wrong in your life, while still being desperate for the companionship of a man. Because by now you have come to realize that there are many men who don't want to be bothered with someone else's children, not that there aren't any exceptions to the rule. But be wary: a man who is eager to be with a woman with small children has to have a pair of eyes fixed on him all of the time! In the court of law, supposedly everyone is innocent until proven guilty. However, in my personal court, if I were a single mother, the law would not apply. I would change the law to reflect my distrust of a man eager to be with me when I have small kids. My new, made-up law, would state "guilty until proven innocent!" The jury will remain out until it can be determined that it is me that he wants, and not my children.

Instead of being desperate for affection and love from a man, see it in your children, your family, and in the friendships that you have. Nothing worth having is easy, life is not easy, but it is good to you when you're good to it. For some of us, we've not been fortunate enough to have the blessing of being born into a healthy family. Every one of us has a certain amount of dysfunction in our lives.

We can't choose the family that we're born into, but we can make a better choice when it comes to choosing the people to share our lives with, including our friends. So start seeing the love in your life, whether it is with the amazing children you have (who didn't ask to be here), your family, or your friendships. Nourish that love and love will come in the ability to see it where it resides, in you.

Emancipation Proclamation of 2011

Desiderata

13

Freedom of Choice

I am a generous person by nature, always have been. If you are a friend or just an acquaintance, I could easily show my gratitude for your being in my life, or doing something special for me, by giving you something in return. I have a friend who once told me that she was told by a friend of hers that she should not be so nice and giving to the men who come into her life. She also said to her that she should get to know them first because she could be taken advantage of. I responded to that by saying that I thought it was perfectly okay for her to be who she was. If she's a giving person, be giving. I told her not change who she was because she's afraid of being taken advantage of.

I can't imagine living in a world where I couldn't be free to be who I am out of fear of how I would be labeled, or treated. If I want to be bighearted, that's what I am going to be. If someone wants to take that as a sign of weakness, or that I am desperate for their affection, then shame on 'em. I believe in being myself and therefore making it easier for people to show themselves for whom they are.

When my husband and I first got together, he said he loved my Isley Brothers CD. I bought him a copy. He couldn't believe my generosity and went on and on about how sweet it was. Obviously, he hadn't had anyone be giving to him in a while. It was simple for me, but it was a big deal to him. I didn't buy it for him to purchase his affection; I got it for him because he liked it. I liked him and I could afford to give it to him. Not once did he take the gift as a sign of my weakness for him. Had he done so, I would have acknowledged it and called him on it, and moved on if it had been necessary to do so.

I have another friend who's in a relationship that she's uncertain about. She questions his every move and spoken word. Sometimes when she talks with him on the phone, she may notice that he hasn't said her name out loud, and she assumes that he does so intentionally because someone, another woman, may be in his presence. When he does this, she questions him about it later. She also says that if she calls him and he doesn't answer when she knows he's there, she'll question him about that. She says he told her that sometimes he'd answer just so that he doesn't have to hear about it later. I told her that it's a shame that he can't have the freedom to show her who he really is.

She's trying desperately to mold the relationship into something that it may not have the capacity for and she may potentially ruin its possibilities because of her insecurities. Not only has she taught him how to treat her, she's taught him how to pretend to be what she needs him to be. If she stops and lets it be what it is going to be, and let him show her who he is, she may be able to weed through the mess and find something there. But like many women who have been hurt, she's afraid to let him show her who he is for fear that she may not like what she sees because she doesn't want to deal with disappointment again. I'd rather see the big-ass elephant and be disappointed, than to find myself years later in a loveless, disrespectful, hurtful, pretentious relationship.

When my husband and I are out, he notices other women. He has the freedom to do so. Why not? I notice other men! To try and take that away from him would be like me trying to make him something that he is not, whereas he is simply what he is; a man. As long as I live, I am fully aware there will always be women more beautiful than myself, and men more handsome than my husband. But if he is in my company and he is indulging in a prolonged stare, it becomes less about noticing her and more about not remembering that I am in his presence. This means that he needs to refocus his attention.

Not only does my husband notice other women, but he also knows other women besides me. How ridiculous would it be for me to be jealous every time he speaks to another woman? Or if when he does speak to one, I ask him, "Who is she?!" Especially if the question was not asked from a place of curiosity, but out of concern for who it is that could potentially be taking my place. My husband had a life before me, and outside of me. It's a shame really. There are many women who are more concerned with what their man is "getting into," rather than what their children are getting into.

Another freedom I believed in and enjoyed (as you know) was my sexual freedom. It's a little different out here in the world because of HIV and such, but when I was younger and single, I did my thang! You know all about the double standard that exists for women who have sex with a man on the first date. And I must admit, there were a few times when I *was* that double standard. So if I liked a guy (not necessarily for his mind) I would make the choice to be with him.

My mother talked a lot to me about the birds and the bees long before the loss of my virginity. She never sugarcoated the act of sex or downplayed it. She was very open with me. She explained to me that if I were to have sex with a guy, to be sure that my choice was because *I* wanted to be with him. I learned not to be with a guy because I thought it would make him like me more. Of course, he may have wanted me more, but it didn't necessarily mean that he wanted more than sex; sex does not equal a relationship. She said everything she could to prepare me for the time that she knew would come to pass.

I listened to what she said and as a result, I was prepared for my first sexual experience; knowledge is freedom and freedom is power. However, even though I experienced my sexual freedom, I made a few mistakes but thankfully, they have not followed me "all the days of my life." I enjoyed myself and tried to be responsible by having rules, which I followed. The one rule I wouldn't break was that I would only be involved with one guy at a time. I didn't want to find myself pregnant, or with a disease, and trying to figure out who the daddy was or how many men I would have to go through to find out who gave who what!

I must confess that I have not always felt a sense of freedom in relationships. I have lost what I considered a good friend because I was not being true to myself. I always thought that the true sign of a friend is a person who allowed a friend to be themselves and in turn, feel comfortable in being themselves around me without fear of being judged. The only problem was, I allowed that friend to define the relationship. I didn't know that was what I was doing. I thought what I was doing was allowing her the freedom to be herself, because I was clear on who I was. I didn't need to be defined by this or any relationship.

The relationship went on for about nine years. I was not unhappy in it, but as time went on it became exhausting to be in a room with her and pretend. When I tried to just be with her and allow my true self to come out, which is passionate, opinionated and self-assured (because during most of the relationship, she was the only one with an opinion, and hers was always right), she would ask me if I was all right. She said that she felt like I was changing, and I could see the look in her eyes reflected concern for how things would affect her. I would reassure her that I was okay, but I could tell that she had her doubts.

When I couldn't take it anymore, I decided to take her out to dinner and talk with her. I really wanted her to respond to me with compassion, but instead she responded to me with derision. She only talked about herself and how she felt hoodwinked. She misunderstood completely. What I had tried to accomplish that evening was to give her insight as to who I really was. I wanted her to know that I was not changing but coming into myself. She was not accepting of it and challenged me every step of the way.

I believe that what she thought was that the dynamics of the relationship would have to change. Even though I was the one with the "problem," her participation was necessary. It meant that she would have to be open to the person that I am. In order for her to be open for me, she would have had to be willing to allow the relationship between us to change, and she was not willing to do so. She was completely satisfied in the relationship because it allowed her to live in her glass house. I didn't want to be a willing participant any longer. I longed for a deeper friendship than that with her. The sad part is that she was, and I'm sure she still is, a beautiful human being. She was just flawed, as we all are. The only difference is that many of us don't mind our imperfections being seen by others.

Freedom of choice is the single most important freedom there is. As a Black woman, I often look at my children and my life with the realization that we (Black women) have not always had the freedom to choose. I think back to generations before me, when our children, just after being born, were taken away from us and sold into the life of bondage.

I was born in 1964 at the start of the Civil Rights Movement. Just one or two generations before mine, my people did not have the right to vote, walk into the front door of an establishment, or drink from the same water fountain as others. And though we were finally allowed an education, our resources were inferior. But it's not just Black women who have felt the sting of subjugation. All women, on some level or another, have been historically oppressed because of culture and stereotypes.

So having said that, I am not interested in giving my freedom to choose to anyone other than myself. I am proud to say that I am a married woman with the freedom of choice. *I* choose who my friends are. *I* choose how to dress my body. *I* make a choice if I want to go shopping. *I* make the choice to be gone all day long, alone or with a friend, without a single call from my husband asking me what to do with the kids, or when am I coming home.

There are women out there in relationships who either don't have the freedom of choice or don't feel comfortable with being able to choose. The latter may be because of the nature of their relationship, which could range from abusive to controlling. I am proud of the freedom I experience in my marriage because I am married to a man who is sure enough of himself and our relationship to have no problem whatsoever with it. However, had he made it difficult for me to have my freedom of choice, it would have been my choice not to be with him.

I was watching *Oprah* one time. It was about women who were either married to or in relationships with pedophiles. One particular segment was about a woman who had traveled many, many miles to start a new life after either a breakup or a divorce, with her two daughters. Very shortly after meeting a new man, he offered her drugs and she partook in the use of them. That was the first clue that something was wrong! Somewhere down the line in their relationship, her three-year-old daughter said to her that he touched her "girlfriend," referring to her private parts. This ridiculous woman convinced herself that her three-year-old daughter was confused about what she was saying. How would a three-year-old be able to articulate such a delicate subject?

She confronted her boyfriend about it and he convinced her, with some tears, that he would never do anything like that. Not long after that, she found her three-year-old daughter in a locked bedroom with the pedophile; he had on the mother's underwear. He was lying in the bed, fondling himself. The precious little girl was naked on the bed next to him, while porn was playing on the television.

She responded to the traumatic experience by killing him stone cold. She and her daughter will have to live with the consequences of *her* choices for the rest of *their* lives. Not only did she choose a man over her daughter, but also killed another human being.

We all make mistakes. And many of us are one mistake (choice) away from changing our future potential, all because we couldn't see the big-ass elephant in the room. The consequences from a choice could be devastating. As devastating as the outcome was for this woman, fortunately for her, she still has the opportunity to go on with her life with some level of normalcy. But there are other women who have made a choice that landed them in jail for life, or with a disease that there is no cure for.

I was one decision away myself from making what could have been the worst mistake of my life. It would have changed the course of my life forever. I once dated a guy (not Lover Boy) who convinced me that he wanted me to have his baby! Yikes!!! I stopped taking my birth control pills for one month. During the course of that month I found out some things that I didn't like about him. Boy, I had never been so happy in all my life when my period came on. What the fuck was I thinking? We dated for a while longer and I pretended that I was still trying to have that baby, and played the part of the frustrated woman when my period came on. I was popping those birth control pills like they were candy.

The potential outcome of that mistake would not have necessarily been the child I could have conceived, but the fact that I would have had to deal with him for the rest of my life, and he was an idiot. In that month's time, I learned what kind of man he truly was. He was a liar and a cheater. I thought he wanted to have a child with me because he loved me. Oh, I was so stupid, I should have known better than that. What he wanted was to have me be a part of his life for all eternity. Not because he loved me, but because he had an unhealthy need to feel like he had power. And getting pregnant by him would have given him just that, a sense of power. Because he would have been able to, on some level, yank my chain as long as that child was a part of my life. I believe he would have never given me a moment of peace!

I am grateful for my experiences, including my choices of men. Let me explain. When I was younger, I did things because I wanted to be closer to the guy in my life. For example, I dated a young man who loved drinking iced tea. I don't like tea, but I tried to learn to because it was what he liked. I wanted to have a connection to him. But what if he was into drugs and encouraged me to do them? What if he was a thug and robbed corner stores? Would I have gotten caught up because I wanted to let him know that I was down? As an adult woman, the answer is a resounding, NO! But as a young woman coming into myself, I didn't know. I'm grateful I never had to find out. In any case, I am confident I would have made a good choice because I'm a quick learner. I don't have to be beat over the head with a sledgehammer in order to get it!

Just because we have the freedom to choose, we still have to be responsible for the choices we make and their consequences. As an adult, parent or wife, any decisions made by us have to be made with our family in mind because of how the result of those decisions can affect the entire family. So it is with this knowledge that we have to live our lives by making the best choices possible, so that the outcomes of those choices do not have harmful consequences. If we come through these experiences unscathed, there will be the opportunity to choose and then to learn from the experience for personal growth. Because as I have said, living is learning!

I started this book off by dissin' and dismissin' the wealth of information out there for women about how to get a man. I can not say anything on the subject at all, so this is my contribution to the cause.

Ladies, as most of you know, it's not hard to find and get a man. The difficult part is finding a good one, and when you find one, keeping him. If you just want a man, drive around the corner and you'll have your pick of any guy standing on the corner. He'll be smoking who knows what, and drinking who knows what, out of a paper bag. He'll be happy to have you because he has nothing else better to do. If he did, he'd be doing it! The sad part to this story is that there are still a lot of women out there willing to settle for this kind of man just to have one.

I hate to break it to you; but how to get a man is more about who you are than who he is. I have a dear friend who, for the life of her, is unable to attract the right kind of man. She still hasn't come to terms with her many issues. Like why she keeps attracting the wrong men, and being so damn picky, when she's no prize herself. Don't get me wrong, because she is a lovely person. But she's flawed in a way that has inhibited her from being able to see the forest for the trees!

She's not willing to see what her issues are; she's too busy looking at his. She has not been able to learn from her mistakes because she continues to think that the men she chooses are all about them being wrong, rather than them being wrong for her. She chooses not to like a man because everything about him is wrong. The way he dresses, what he drives, or what he does for a living. Not the important things, like the fact that he may be a good listener, considerate, generous and respectable. She always wants the man who has made himself unavailable to her.

There is nothing wrong with her wanting to have a man in her life, but it seems that she is looking for the perfect man. However, in order to get that perfect man, she would have to be that perfect woman. And perfect she is not! No one is perfect. My wish is that she would, rather than look for his level of perfection, judge him based on his dependability.

How to keep a man starts first with how you got him. So be careful how you get him, because the same way you got him, someone else can, too. If you got him by "stealing" him from someone else, he can be easily stolen from you as well. But even that very statement is full of problems in and of itself. You can't steal someone from someone. In order for a person to be taken from another, they would have had to make themselves available, which would mean that they've left the other person of their own free will.

Like I said, a man must be in a relationship of his own free will and not because there is always an overt effort to keep him interested. Otherwise it becomes something that can't be depended on. A woman who would do such a thing will always feel like she has to ante up. In the end, it is not going to matter how much it took to keep him. How much money she kept in his pocket. How good she kept him dressed. How much more beautiful she is, or how much better she thinks her pussy is.

When I was single and found myself attracted to a man who

was unreceptive to my advances, I thought it meant that he was the one with the problem. I thought he was either gay or pussy whipped. If I had allowed myself to see it any other way, I would have realized that it was me with the problem. Because I couldn't imagine a man ever turning down pussy that was free! His turning me down had nothing to do with me, nor did he have a problem. He may have just been satisfied in his life. Or maybe, I wasn't his type. I know now that if a man doesn't have an attraction toward me, that's okay. Every man doesn't have to want me; I don't want every man.

The real issue was that I had my eyes set on a particular guy. He didn't reciprocate; he was already involved with another woman. I refused to accept that he would turn *me* down. In my mind, if anyone deserved to have a man being faithful to her, then it would be me. But instead what I got was rejection. And because of it, I wanted to prove to myself that happily ever after didn't exist, because if it did, *I* would have it!

There are several key ways to keeping a man and the first one lays in your ability to live your life without him, and his awareness of that fact. My husband knows that I love him and that I would kiss his ass and the ground that he walks on. But I am also willing to tell him how I feel or what I think about something, whether he likes it or not. I don't live in fear of him not liking what I have to say because it could make him decide that he wants to make himself available to be "stolen."

I remember several years ago he got some tickets to go to a professional basketball game. I'm minimally interested in sports, and he knows that. I was at work when he asked if I'd go to the game with him. My co-worker overheard my end of the conversation when I told him "no." She proceeded to tell me, "You should go to the game with that man," as if he was someone she needed to pity, and that I should have been grateful to have a man who would want to take me to a ball game. What she was probably thinking is that I had better go to the game because other women would be there.

She only heard one side of the conversation; mine. He was neither disappointed nor put off by the fact that I decided not to go to the game. My husband and I share many interests, and a few that we don't. But he didn't (and still doesn't) need me to go to a ball game with him to make his life complete. If he really wanted me to go, he would have said he really wanted me to go and I would have gone. He ended up asking one of his friends to go with him and they had a great time.

Another key to keeping a man has mostly to do with your ability to let him be! It's amazing how many men act as though women are a thorn in their sides or their balls and chains. And you know why; many of us are the anchors in the relationship. I don't mean anchor as in stability. I mean an anchor as in burden. We can be so needy; damn!

There are probably many women out there who will not agree with what I am about to say, but I am going to say it anyway. Ladies, please let your man go to the strip club! What is he going to do? Maybe get a hard-on, so what?! Supposedly, men are not to touch the women, and hopefully he won't. But what if he does? (And by no means take this to mean that I am okay with any man putting his hands on a woman who is not his. Because any man who would do such a thing is just a man who doesn't value what he has at home.) It would be wrong and if you found out about it, deal with it, but *IT WOULD NOT BE THE END OF THE WORLD, AS YOU KNOW IT. LIFE WILL GO ON, AND SO WILL YOU!* What is the difference between a man going to a strip club and a woman going to a male strip club? I don't know about you, but if I choose to go, I love the idea that I have the freedom of choice.

What could you be afraid of? That another woman can turn him on? So what! As long as you live, there will always be more beautiful women than yourself. I am not the finest woman in the world, but my husband didn't marry me because of my ass. He married me because of my chicken salad!

I talked about how to keep him, but let me go back for a moment and suggest another way of getting him. It is simpler than you probably think. **TELL HIM!** Make your presence known. You can't know how many grown women I have heard say that they were pining over some man but were afraid to tell him so. What is there to be afraid of? My time is very precious to me; I wouldn't want to spend it by pining over someone who may not feel the same. If he doesn't feel the same, I would find something else to do with my time, like forgetting about him.

I had a supervisor many years ago on another job. She was hell in that position. When I say that she gave everybody grief, I mean it. It would be mostly for no reason at all or just because she could. Once, a few of us ladies were on a break and she was discussing how she was infatuated with a guy that she had been having sex with, but she was afraid to let him know how besotted she was. Now mind you, she was a divorced single parent of three children. I told her that I couldn't understand how a woman, having had sexual experiences, and having had children (children that not only came from her womb, but also from between her legs) could be nervous about telling him how she felt! Those qualifications alone should have been enough for her to have the gumption necessary to tell him how she felt.

It made no sense to me that she gave us hell at work, but she tried to pretend to be shy around him. It also made no sense that she could feel comfortable with sleeping with him, but not in telling him how she felt. Talk about an oxymoron. Who was she trying to fool, him, or the ones whom she told that cockamamie story to? If I had to guess, I would say it was the latter.

I am sure he didn't think she was sleeping with him to pass the time away. He probably knew she was with him because she was hoping for more with him. But who was he to complain; he had it going on. It cost him nothing to have her the way he wanted her, and he used it to his advantage because it was uncomplicated. Who knows, it could have been an arrangement that she agreed to, but had a change of heart, and was unwilling to test the waters by risking rejection.

It is perfectly okay to tell a man how you feel. I have done it, and I have been rejected. Yes, my ego was bruised when I was rejected because I thought, why wouldn't he want to be with me? But it never had anything to do with me. Even if the reason for the rejection was because I was not his type; it still had nothing to do with me. Rather, it was about what he wanted for himself. As I have already stated, I didn't want every man who wanted to be with me, so what would make me think that every man I wanted would want to be with me?

When I asserted myself with men, I may not have ended up with a long-term relationship, but I sometimes got something else out of the process: a temporary lover, which ended up suiting me fine. You can find out a lot about a man when you have sex with him; particularly that he may not be the one you want to take home to meet your mama. Being assertive resulted in the union between my husband and me. If I had waited on him to make a move, I may have still been waiting.

Did you notice that the word I chose to use is *assertion*, not *aggression*? There is a big difference between the two. To be assertive means to go after what you want with a certain amount of confidence. But with aggression, think of a pit bull. It's like being relentless when going after something. I don't mind letting a man know how I feel about him, but to go after him when he has made himself clear about not wanting me is to punish him, and myself. Why would I want to waste my precious time going after a man who doesn't want me? Like I said, my time is very precious to me. I don't even like wasting too much time waiting my turn at the salon, but I have no other choice. It's not like I can do my own hair. So if you want someone who doesn't want you, find something else to do with your time until you find someone else who is worthy of the time you can give him.

Ultimately, the key to keeping a man is to get YOU together first. Stop acting like you don't know which way is up. If you don't have a clue, start by hanging out with some people who have some sense, or get some therapy. Because of the poor job that's been done of raising our boys, you will no doubt find yourself in a relationship with one of them. Then where will the two of you be?

You could meet a man with potential to be greater than what he could imagine, and he will be totally lost if you don't know what you are doing. But by no means take this to mean that you are responsible for how men are; it's just that with the pickings of real men out there being so slim, you have to be able to identify if he is decent and has the potential to be a great partner.

If you invest in yourself and become the person you were meant to be, when you meet a man who is worthy of your time, you'll be ready for the challenge. Because if he has a sense of decency about him, and you are who you need to be, it won't be like the blind leading the blind. There is nothing worse than one stupid person giving advice to another stupid person!

If you have a man and you've kept him, he's still there for one or more of seven reasons:

1. He has nothing else better to do or nowhere else to be.
2. You have nothing else better to do or nowhere else to be.
3. You are maybe in a relationship in which you feel afraid, or feel the inability to leave because of abuse, your children, or your finances.
4. You feel he is the best you could get.
5. You think you're in love.
6. The sex is mind-blowing!
7. Or he's worth it!

Women stay in relationships for many reasons. They are sometimes self-sacrificing, and the sacrificing is sometimes necessary for many reasons. But only you know the reason you choose to stay in a dysfunctional relationship. And if it's for any reason other than because he's worth it, then you may be wasting your time. If you didn't notice, I didn't say because you love him. As Tina Turner says, *"What's love got to do, got to do with it?"* It has nothing to do with it!

If you were a single mother and the man in your life took really good care of you and your children, not just financially, but maybe spiritually, would you choose not to be with him just because you didn't love him? My mother says, "A woman don't have to love that man, but that man has got to love that woman." She believes, and I believe as well, that you could learn to love a man who takes care of your person. Only, of course, if he looks like an ogre, then you have some negotiating to do. At that point you have to decide what is more important to you; someone who treats you well, or someone who is good to look at. Sometimes the ones that are the best looking are either capable of beating your ass, or are thinking only of what's in it for them. But ultimately, it's up to you, and what you want for yourself. Because, ladies, we are the ones who set the tone in the relationship we have with our men.

It can never be emphasized enough how important dress is. If you were to go on a job interview, in order to be taken seriously, you have to dress the part. It would mean being dressed appropriately from head to toe for the job you're interviewing for. It would also mean you need to be clean and neat, with makeup natural looking, perfume and jewelry kept to a minimum. In addition to your attire, it is important that you have good interviewing skills. The same applies if you are looking to be taken seriously in your personal life.

I have said before and I repeat, this book is not about how to get a man, but again, I have to say my piece: IF YOU WANT TO BE TAKEN SERIOUSLY (by a man), DRESS THE PART! If you want a serious relationship, you have to be taken seriously. If you want to be taken seriously, you have to first be perceived as serious. You have to be serious about what it is that you want.

Every book is judged by its cover. Knowing that this is true, why do so many women decide to leave absolutely nothing to the imagination? Don't get me wrong, you should accentuate your best attributes, but that doesn't mean you should subject yourself and others to the results of your overexposing yourself. If you have beautiful legs, wear a short skirt. And by this I mean not one that is short enough to expose your ischial tuberosity (the lower part of your pelvic bone). If you are nicely endowed, show some cleavage, not enough that an accident could cause some spillage, especially if it is intended; it's not ladylike. And for goodness sake, if you are heavily endowed, invest in a good bra.

My mother used to always say to me when I was younger, "Stop trying so hard to be seen. No matter who you are or what you do, someone has their eyes on you." Once again, she was right. Most of the attention I have received was when I didn't even notice that anyone cared. The guy I lost my virginity to had been noticing me for quite some time, and I wasn't aware of it. Our first conversation revealed all of the things he knew about me. He knew where I lived, where I went to school and the route by which I traveled when I walked to see my big sister. He had taken some time to get to know me before he actually introduced himself to me. I don't know if that is a good thing or not, but at any rate, he was at least harmless. He had already formed an opinion of me just by noticing me. It took our first conversation for him to better decide if he liked me as much up close as he did from afar.

Children sometimes act out to get attention. Some do so out of a need to gain attention, whether the attention is good or bad. The same could be said of a woman who dresses in inappropriately revealing ways. She does so to get attention by any means necessary. The problem is, what she will get is the type of attention that will not last beyond that moment. A man would only be interested because of what it is he thinks his sexual gain would be.

As a woman, if I were looking for a man, he'd have to have more than a job and a place to live, as a qualification, for me to take him seriously. He doesn't even necessarily have to have his own place as long as he is taking care of his business, in an effort to have more for the future.

If he doesn't have a job, it would have to be because he has resources, as in family money, and is living his life with maturity. If he were a full-time college student, he would have to be taking his education seriously. But he certainly couldn't be walking around here in jeans halfway down his ass. I am a forty-seven-year-old woman, and I wouldn't want to be with a man who dresses like my son would want to. He can't be riding around in a car with wheels that cost more than the car. If it quacks like a duck…it doesn't make any sense; it shows where his priorities lie, or his lack thereof.

The same can be said for women who dress inappropriately. How could a real man take her seriously if she's dressed like a hoochie mama? He can't. He will only be interested in her for as long as it takes to get what he wants from her, some hooch. And I am not talking about the kind you drink. She also would not be the woman he would want to take home to meet his mama.

It doesn't matter how physically fine you are. If you have a body like Beyoncé's, it still needs to be dressed appropriately. I am no small woman. I have curves, and some of them are where I wish they weren't. I personally have no interest in putting a garment on my body that is not made for it. Even if it fits, it needs to be age-appropriate; not just because of my size, but because I am a mother. Don't get me wrong, I like to look hot and dress sexy, as well. And I do, when I want to prove something to myself.

However, I have nothing to prove to anyone else. And I certainly don't need a man's validation of me to determine whether I am worth a glance from him, or for him to show me that he knows what is sexy about me. Sexiness, first and foremost, is a state of mind, with appearance being secondary. Secondly, I am a mother; I don't want my children to look at me and be embarrassed about my appearance because I am trying to be something that I am not; young and hip. I am seasoned, mature and aware. My self-assurance comes from my ability to know my limitations.

Cat Fight

15

One of the ongoing problems that still seem to plague us women is how we treat one another. It is an awful shame that we cannot have enough mutual love and respect for one another with all of our shared life experiences, good and bad, with our children, men, careers, etc. Women can be so judgmental toward other women, even when they know their own shit stinks. My mother used to say, in response to women judging another woman's circumstances, "If she don't understand, it's because she's either never been there, or she's lying." It's easy to sit back and point the finger at someone else's situation; especially when there is no understanding of what another woman is going through. If she's never been there, it's because she's never been in the same situation, or she's too busy pretending that her circumstances are above everyone else's.

I don't ever remember a time in my grown-up, adult life when I didn't like someone for no reason at all. But I have lost female friends for no apparent reason or have had women roll their eyes at me for the same reason. I can remember, however, when I was in college and I slept with this guy (yeah, I thought he was cute) just because I didn't like his girlfriend! If I didn't mention it, I was young and I thought I had a good reason; I thought she was arrogant!

Now, how *stupid* was that, to think that she thought she was better than me? I had never even had a conversation with her, so where did I get that idea? And what difference did it make, even if she did think that way? None. In the end, it wasn't even worth it. It may have been worth it if the sex was good, but it wasn't. Not only that, but I can't even remember his name. I am not sure if that last statement is funny or sad. If it is either, who is the funny or sad one? Him because his "actions" were forgettable, or me because I had made a stupid choice? What is unfortunate is that we still have that kind of carrying-on with women in their thirties, forties, and fifties.

When we get to a certain age, with our many experiences, we're supposed to become more mature. Some folks' definition of maturity is holding down a job, having babies, and paying bills. It all boils down to the ability of us being able to be happy with ourselves. I'm not talking about how we look, dress, where we live, what we drive or what we do for a living. I accept that I will never be a size 6 or live in a mansion with someone at my beck and call.

I am not saying that either isn't possible. But in the instance of my being a size 6, if I were to be a size 6, because it does not come natural for me, it would take more than what I am willing to give up (at this point in my life) to achieve it. Not only that, but my head is too big for it; I would look like a bobble head. But neither am I jealous of someone who has all of those things. The grass is not always greener on the other side. And besides, there will always, as long as we live, be taller, skinnier, prettier, richer people than ourselves (and vice versa).

It doesn't make any sense to be jealous of someone because you perceive her to have something that is desirable. I know, of course, that that doesn't keep us from being sometimes envious. It doesn't make sense because whatever it is they have, that which you'd like for yourself, they may have to earn every bit of it. However, it is important that you understand everyone has a story. And sometimes you don't always realize what it is that you're jealous of when you're jealous of it.

Imagine a woman married to a rich man. She may never have to worry about money and how her bills are paid ever again, but you don't know what she has to put up with in order to have that life. She may have to earn every penny! For all you know he may be aware that she married him for his money and he uses it to his advantage, to get what he wants from her. She may not have the freedom that you enjoy because she's on a leash, and it may be a very short one. On the other hand, he may love her dearly and shower her with gifts. And if that is so, so what? It's her life; get your own!

I have been overweight my entire adult life; in one way or another. My heaviest was after I had my first child; my baby girl. I remember though, before she was a notion, my husband, compared to me, was more than a lowercase version of me and fairly good-looking. Once, he personally brought me two-dozen roses at my job in celebration of Valentine's Day. I heard someone made the comment, "That's *her* husband? How did she get him?!" As if to insinuate that someone that looked like me could never get a man that looked like him. I had to assume that it may have been because she thought that if anyone deserved to have a man bring her beautiful flowers on "lover's day," and a good-looking one at that, it was her.

She was a spectator to my relationship with him. All she knew was what she saw. My husband was a good person, but she didn't know that. I could have been catching hell for all she knew. She judged us from our external appearance, as though he was the prize, not me!

I have experienced this sort of treatment at other times. My husband and I purchased our first home while we were in the honeymoon phase of our relationship. Our next-door neighbor was a woman. She was extremely cordial to my husband, but made every attempt to make me feel like an outsider to the relationship she tried to have with him by not acknowledging my presence.

We ran into her at the grocery store a few times. Once, I noticed her talking to him at the end of the aisle. Her body language suggested that they were engaged in a very "funny" conversation. I saw her laughing and slapping her knees while "patting" him on the shoulder. When the conversation was over, she walked down the aisle toward me and looked me dead in my eyes without saying a word (she did that, ignored me, whenever he and I were together).

What was she trying to accomplish? And why was it necessary? I assume that she had nothing else better to do! Was she attempting to make me feel insecure by trying to appear as though there was something going on between the two of them? I can't be sure. But what I do know is that not even that stunt was enough for me to unpack my luggage and hand over my insecurities, if I had any, to my husband and make it about him not respecting me.

Don't get me wrong; I made sure he understood how I felt about her and what she was doing, and about him for not noticing. But it was not his fault she was being a bitch! What he ended up doing to rectify the situation was continue to be pleasant with her while keeping his distance.

Another way women hate on one another is the relationship between themselves and their daughter, with their man's children from another relationship, or with baby mama drama. It is unfortunate, but there are some young ladies who experience jealousies from an unlikely source; their mothers. It's appalling! Mothers are supposed to be their children's go-to person, the people that can make anything happen from nothing. I have heard stories of how mothers are jealous of their daughter's good looks or opportunities. Any mother who is not sympathetic or encouraging to her own offspring is beyond any description I could imagine. The only thing I can come up with is frightening!

I was fortunate to marry a man without children. But had he had children, I could've never done something that would encourage him not to have a relationship with them. If I had done so, how dare I act as though the only children that matter are the ones that I birthed?! Some women's goal is to block the man from having communication with the mama and they may do it via the children. Unfortunately, the children are the ones who suffer. If that other woman is calling and being rude, it's because she's been allowed to be rude, by him. So then you, the new woman in his life, become rude with her and it becomes something altogether different from what it was supposed to be about; the child. That's like finding your man in bed with another woman and you want to whip her ass. His ass is the one that deserves to be whipped.

If you are a woman who is in a relationship with a man that has children from a previous relationship, it will be full of challenges. It can be challenging because of the children's attitudes, or because of baby mama drama syndrome. There are relationships that have ended on a good note, with or without children involvement. But when children are involved, the challenges faced are less difficult to manage only when everyone involved is on the same page.

If you are having baby mama drama, you need to leave it alone and let your man deal with it. It becomes a bigger problem when he decides to do nothing about it, or when you think it is your responsibility to get her in check. You will have resentment from his baby mama. She will be angry because she thinks that you have taken her place or are taking something away from her children; their father. Complacency from him will emerge because you are fighting a battle that is not yours to fight or because it's not important to him. If there is baby mama drama, it most likely has nothing to do with you. If you are asserting yourself by placing yourself right in the middle of it, it will be because you want his baby mama to respect your place in his life. But that can't be done until *he* respects your place in his life!

When she calls the house and doesn't respect you, don't talk to her. If you're in a serious relationship with him, he should know the kind of woman you are and your expectations of him in the relationship. Give him the phone and let him deal with her. He has to set up rules, which she has to follow. If she can't follow them, she shouldn't be allowed to call the house. If he can't enforce them, you may need to rethink your choice in men. Because his actions would be symptomatic of him not being serious about the life he wants with you.

Years ago my husband received a phone call from a female. She attempted to sound sexy over the phone when asking to speak with him. I called his name out and told him he had a phone call. I instantly knew that someone was trying to play games, but I didn't have time for that kind of childishness. He talked to this person for probably ten to twenty minutes. When he finished the conversation, he told me that it was a childhood friend's little sister. She was in town with her school's choir for a concert and it was her intention to see my husband while she was in town. He was like an uncle to her. I found it entertaining, because she was a young lady by this time, either in her late-teens or early twenties, trying to play games with someone that invented them.

I told my husband that when she called and asked to speak to him, she didn't identify herself or acknowledge me when I answered the phone. I also told him what she sounded like on the phone. He was upset, because she was a little girl playing stupid games on the phone, intentionally trying to cause problems.

Later that evening, when she called back, my husband put her on front street. He asked her if she knew that it was his wife that answered the phone. Her response was "yes." He then asked her why she didn't say hello to me; I can't remember what her response was. But he went on to say to her that the next time she ever called his house, or anyone's house, that she needed to be polite by saying hello to the person who answers the phone. And if they don't know who she is, she should identify herself. He embarrassed her because she thought she was being cute. I know that it was because she probably didn't like me after hearing the false stories that were circulating about me throughout his entire family! In any case, she never pulled another stunt like that again. As a matter of fact, I don't think she's ever called our house again.

It was not my position to get into a phone fight with this little girl. She was acquainted with my husband, not me, and therefore he needed to handle it. Had he not, I would have considered it an indication that he didn't take what we had seriously. And as for women that are having baby mama drama syndrome, the only thing that will be accomplished, by getting into a phone fight with his baby mama, is the two of you trying to antagonize each other. You, because you want to let her know that you have something that she wants: him. Her, because she wants you to know she has something you don't, his child, and therefore an everlasting connection to him. When it gets to this point, everyone has forgotten what is the most important thing: the child.

When it comes time for him to pick up his children, and she tries to make you feel left out, then don't go. She shouldn't have the power to make you feel left out, anyway. He does. But if she makes things difficult by playing silly games, if you do go, stay in the car! Don't get in the middle of something just because you want to prove to her that he is your man now. If you've got to do all of that to have a relationship with him, then it's not worth it unless you like being in the middle of drama.

But as I mentioned earlier, sometimes the battle that exists doesn't always exist between the two women; sometimes it can be with the children from a previous relationship. What kind of woman is it that wouldn't be supportive of her man having a relationship with his children? Insecure, selfish, immature, and basically, a rotten one! Now how does that look? A full grown-ass woman jealous of an underaged person! Outrageous! What are you afraid of? That if he spends time with his children, he also may spend time with the ex? Maybe. Even if the children are old enough and able to manipulate their daddy and steer him away from you, then maybe he is not the man for you; that alone speaks volumes as to his character.

Women can cheat themselves by not having friendships with other women. How many women do you know who don't have female friends because they're afraid to have another woman be anywhere in the vicinity of their man? I have some great friendships, but I am still looking for my "Gayle King." And I know she's out there!

It is sad, but when it comes to women and their men, it's like the "crabs in the barrel" syndrome. We have become programmed to think that because of the low men-to-women ratio, we have to do any and everything to get him and keep him. But not allowing yourself to experience the wonder of having someone who you can tell your secrets to, share a life-changing event with, or go out shopping for hours with, is a shame. As with problems with children from a previous relationship or baby-mama drama, when the relationship between a woman and her man is solid, and she is the mature, self-assured woman she wants to be both within and outside of the relationship, then she will have nothing to worry about.

16

Best Friends Forever (BFF)

It never ceases to amaze me, but there are people out there who believe that men and women can be friends! Now, by no means am I suggesting that it isn't possible, because there is always an exception to any rule. I just don't happen to know of any personally. The word *friend* has been misrepresented, misused and abused. When a man and woman are friends, someone is either thinking about having some sex, or having a relationship.

Even when a woman knows that man is not available for her, she'll call their relationship a friendship just so that she can be in his life by any means necessary. How can you be friends really, if the idea of having something more, or something different, is in your head? You can't! I'm not saying you can't be friendly toward one another. But when there is an ulterior motive, it changes the dynamics of the so-called friendship.

Some women would argue that I am wrong, and it's possible; like I said, I just don't know of any personally. I'm also not saying that I don't have male friends. But if they were to be my friend, it would be because they are also my husband's friends. Before I was married, I had a few male "friends." We were friends because at some point the idea of taking the "friendship" further existed, that is, the desire for a sexual relationship (felt by either him or me) was involved. If I had continued the relationship with a man such as that, how could my husband be comfortable with me having a relationship with a man that I once had sex with? It could be argued that "what he doesn't know won't hurt him," but I wouldn't want my man having an outside "friendship" with a woman that he had once bedded? It is just an opportunity to fill up Pandora's box.

I remember calling myself some guy's friend only because I wanted more than a friendship. How can I be his friend truly if I had an ulterior motive? Because I had romantic feelings for him, I couldn't be objective. I was envious when another woman came sniffing around him. When I saw that, I stopped playing around and told him how I felt. He was not able to give me what I wanted and it changed us forever. And that was okay for me because, even though we continued to be friendly with one another, I stopped pining over him. He was able to move on to the next girl, who could give him what he wanted. And the only kind of relationship that he wanted was the no-strings-attached kind.

Lover Boy and I cohabitated for a short time; the beginning of the end started when he came to me saying that he didn't want to live with me anymore. He also said that we could be "friends." Again, I was young and wanted to believe him. Because if I believed that, then I would also believe that we would get back together after he got over his "phase," like he said we would. We didn't get back together, thank GOD!

On another note, I grew up with a male friend who lived down the street from me. I knew him from the time I moved into the neighborhood as a kid, in the sixth grade. We experienced many things together as friends. He was the first one that I smoked weed with, and the last! As we grew up together and became adults, the relationship changed.

He had been intimate with a friend of mine, and as if that weren't enough, he started to come on to me. I was never interested in him like that; he was like a brother to me, but he didn't care. It started off with him being silly and always making sexual comments or jokes. He was always pushing the envelope, but I wouldn't accept it.

As time went on, if I became involved with a guy, he would always have something negative to say about him. Most of the time, he was right. But his intentions were self-serving. Years had gone by since I saw him when he came back to town with his girlfriend and youngest son. It was during the time of my engagement to my now husband. That time, he criticized many aspects of my relationship with my fiancé, but I quickly put him in his place.

I put him in his place first of all because I knew of his intentions. I was not the same unsure, immature young woman that he left behind. He was testing me to see if he could make me feel insecure about the relationship. He was the kind of person that, if he detected any sense of vulnerability, he would use it as an opportunity to pounce on me and show me how much more than me he knew about everything; especially people. Secondly, I suspect he was spiteful of the life I was leading, because he was not living his life to its fullest potential. If it quacks like a duck... because if he loved me, as I thought he did, he would have been happy for me and voiced any reservations that he had about my upcoming nuptials in a loving and encouraging way.

I made damn sure that he knew his place. He may have been an old "friend," but I was in the process of changing my life, my future. I was in love with my fiancé and he needed to know that he didn't have the power to influence any decisions that I was to be making.

I mentioned how he was the first and the last person that I smoked weed with. I smoked it the first time with him because I had always trusted him like a brother, even though he always made fun of me by calling me an "L 7." If you don't know what that means, it means a "square." I will admit that I was slow to learn about people and their intentions, but he got me started on my journey toward becoming intuitive about people's intentions and this was because of what he did to me.

One night way back when (during my college days), a female friend of mine, he and I went out riding for the night. We went to the waterfront and smoked a joint. Within a few minutes I could tell that something was different. The view from my eyes became very glassy and wavy. I started to feel myself panic and I asked him what was in it. He thought it was amusing to see me in my animated state. But my girlfriend looked at me with widened eyes and started to be upset at what she saw in me. Because I could see how she looked at me, I knew my anxiety would have escalated had I not found a way to hold it together.

I outwardly calmed down and told her that I was okay, but on the inside I was going nuts. I came up with an excuse and had them take me to my sister's house so I could sleep it off. I was in no condition to drive home in that state. I was very angry with him because he put me in a place of defenselessness and I told him so on the next day. I learned my lesson. From that night on, I have never taken another drug unless it was over-the-counter or prescribed by a physician.

My husband was married briefly before we got together. During our courtship, I learned from him that he had been communicating with his ex-wife by phone. Before we married he had some things to take care of. He had to move from a one-bedroom to a two-bedroom apartment to accommodate all of our things. I also gave him a few tasks to do. I had him change his phone number to an unlisted one. I asked him to have a conversation with her to let her know that his life was changing and that conversations between them would have to cease. Whether he had the conversation with her or not, I am not sure, but she has not been a part of our life since our marriage. For all I know, he could have lied to me and said they were talking so he could detect jealousy in me.

I have no doubt that if she had been having conversations with him as he said, then it is because she was attempting to get back with him. In my eyes, they should have nothing to talk about. They no longer shared anything; no real estate or children.

It would have only been a problem if he refused to oblige my request. His refusal would have signified his putting me, and my feelings, behind his need to have her as his "friend," and thus inviting problems with me as his new wife. It would have been an alarm sounding *LOUDLY* in my ear—*DON'T MARRY HIM!* Because I would have taken it to mean that he didn't take me, or our relationship, seriously enough to end it with someone that he couldn't stay married to!

Lose the Luggage.
Don't Be a Bag Lady!

17

Women! Women! We have sooo much baggage! And we have the nerve to pack it up (neatly) and bring it in to the middle, not just the foyer, but smack dab in the middle of any and every room of a new relationship. It is a self-esteem issue that we have unsuccessfully dealt with. Lose that luggage! It is not the same as being stranded in a city where the airport has lost everything essential for a wonderful vacation or successful business trip. The luggage I am referring to is the heavy loads of burdens, disappointments and heartaches we bring to a new relationship. Get rid of it. This is the only luggage that you should be happy to never see again. Without it, you can have a wonderful and successful trip in life.

You have heard me harp on this same subject for just about this entire book. But, let me say it again. YOUR EXPERIENCES ARE FOR YOU TO LEARN FROM, TO GROW FROM. STOP TRYING TO CHANGE THEM—THEY ARE YOUR BLESSING. THEY ARE THERE FOR YOU TO BE CHANGED BY!

Being alive means that we have survived something! Even healthy newborn babies survive coming from what is considered for them a very soothing, calm and warm environment, and are traumatized by being overstimulated in a new world. But guess what? They adjust. We adults become traumatized from our past hurts and allow our past relationships to dictate our future relationships. If a man has done you wrong, it is no reason to be paranoid by believing that every man in your future will have the same plan in mind for you. It also doesn't mean that you shouldn't be aware of another's intention and of what is happening right in front of your eyes. Remember that big-ass elephant? Pay attention to it when it appears in the room.

My husband is the first serious relationship that I got into after I was left broken-hearted by Lover Boy. I had not seen him in ten years since graduating high school. We had begun planning our high school reunion when he and I became reunited. We started a long distance courtship during the planning process.

On the first night of the reunion (get acquainted night), it was a long night for us, especially for me. My then boyfriend, now husband, suggested that he could take me back home. His plan was to come back and hang out with his old classmates for a little while longer. I looked at him like he was crazy! I remember vividly saying to him, "Why do you need to come back?" Of course, I said it with an attitude, with one hand on my hip! From the look in his eyes, I could tell he wasn't quite sure why I was so hostile. His response to me was simply, "You said you were tired and ready to go." That was true. I did say that I was tired. He went on to say that he wasn't tired and he wasn't ready to end the night hanging out and talking with classmates whom he hadn't seen or spoken to in over ten years!

At that moment I realized that I brought the disappointment and pain that I had experienced with Lover Boy into this new and unexplored relationship. I didn't even give him a minute to show me what kind of man he was. I tried to change the experience to suit my needs!

I went on ahead and let him take me home. I took a shower and got in my bed for the night. He came back at about 3 or 4 in the morning just like he said he would. We had a wonderful night and have been together ever since. I gave him room to be himself, to be his own person. I dealt with my past hurts and disappointments by having a present and future with him through not being paranoid, but living in reality. When he said that he wanted to spend more time with his classmates, that's what he meant! But what I heard him saying was that he wanted to spend more time with his classmates, without me, so he could find someone else to cozy up to!

It was truly in that moment that I realized I had tried to bring my baggage right in the middle of the relationship. I attempted to unpack it, but decided to close it up and keep it in the foyer. By keeping it in the foyer (of my mind), I remembered my past only so as not to repeat it in my present and my future. As a matter of fact, my luggage has remained packed up neatly in the foyer ever since. My husband, thankfully, has given me no reason to unpack it!

Talk to Him

18

You can find out a lot about the man in your life if you were to just simply *talk to him*! How in the hell can you get involved in a relationship with someone and not know a thing about them or their past? Don't allow the relationship to exist between the two of you because it is of his choosing. You need to know more about the person to whom you have decided to give access to your stuff!

If you are currently in a relationship, don't you want to know why your man's previous relationship failed? You should be able to talk with him openly about it! If you can't, you may need to find yourself another man. It could be another way of him controlling the situation. It could be because he has the same fate in store for you, or because he has something to hide. It could simply be because he was broken-hearted and bringing it up is too much for him. But if this is the case, then he doesn't need to be in a relationship with you. Because he still isn't over the pain of it all, which means, he still ain't over *her*. Which also means that if she were to come back to him, you're history. Or it could simply mean that he needs to grow up and let go of his baggage!

When my husband and I started dating, we both had the same impression of each other; we each thought the other was awesome. We both also had the same thing on our minds: *Why are you available?* In each of our minds, we thought: *If you are so great, why did someone else let you get away?* The answer was simple for each of us. I was heartbroken by an asshole, and he ended it with a woman he said he didn't love, as he should have.

If you don't know your man's past, you can't know your future with him. We women need to start taking the time to get to know the people to whom we are giving an inside access to our lives and family. I am guilty myself. Hindsight is 20/20. I can see clearly now the many mistakes of my past.

Lover Boy couldn't have gotten as close to me as he had if I had allowed myself to question the fact that he didn't like answering questions about his previous relationship. I felt satisfied in the fact that he didn't feel comfortable talking about it. It was the excuse he made to me. I thought he was showing maturity by not speaking poorly about someone. In reality, he knew it was what he had planned for me: that I would soon be history!

Most of us only want the comfort of being in a relationship with a man who embraces us, and our presence, in every aspect of his life. And yes, I judged a man as boyfriend material by how much freedom and personal space he gave me in our life together. If I were dating a man and it was understood that we were exclusive, then I expected, as I should, to have the ability to answer his phone and knock at his door. If I didn't have that freedom, I knew something wasn't right. If it quacks like a duck…like I said, things are supposed to make sense and when they don't, something is not right.

No More Drama

19

I absolutely hate drama. The only time I think it should rear its ugly head is when you have to defend yourself or a loved one in a situation that couldn't be dealt with in any other way. Sometimes it is a necessary evil. However, there are people I know who seem to only be able to deal with life, on a daily basis, with drama as its requirement. It's too much!

Having drama in your life is a choice—same as if you were to choose what to eat for a snack. You can choose to have potato chips or an apple. If you were trying to keep the weight off, you would choose the better option of the two. If you want peace in your life, you should make the choice to eliminate or alter the things that cause the drama in your life.

Pun intended—drama is a scene-stealer. It takes the focus off of the real issue and makes it about who can be the most ridiculously animated in order to gain the most attention so they can have their own way. It generally solves nothing, because nothing is gained from it. It just leads to more drama.

Drama happens because the people who live in it do so because they don't know how to deal with their problems, or because they don't care to deal with them. Drama also happens when a person likes to see chaos all around them; making others feel insecure. It gives them a sense of control and makes them feel superior.

Gossip and rumors are a source of drama. As I mentioned a few times before, the environment on most jobs is just like a soap opera. In that soap opera one finds people who are the instigators of rumors and gossip. People who start rumors are the unhappiest of people. Without a doubt, I believe that a person who is happiest with himself is a person who derives no pleasure from seeing another suffer.

Like most everyone else, I have been gossiped about. It is a fate that probably none of us will be able to escape. People will always have something to say about nothing. You can't control it because some people believe what they want to believe, not what is true. If you drove around in a bright shiny new car, some will say, "She thinks she is something special just because she has a new car." If the car was a hooptie, those same people will say, "Look at her riding around in that junk car." You can't win! You'll be judged one way or another.

Just because I've been the source of gossip doesn't mean that I have to know about it. Once a co-worker attempted to tell me what someone said to them about me, and I am sure that it was told to her in the strictest of confidence. I promptly let her know that I was not interested in hearing about it. I didn't want to know.

First of all, who's to say that she was accurate about the information that she was about to give me? She could have been completely mistaken about what someone else said. It could have been misinterpreted. Second, she could have been lying about that same information. Thirdly, her intentions probably were solely to make me feel insecure about something that may or may not have been said, and thus making the drama continue.

Drama can also exist in our home lives. When my husband and I used to argue, he did a lot of yelling. It was what he was used to. Yelling to me is a form of drama. I never understood the need for it. He yelled because it was his way of trying to control the situation (or me). I believe that two rational people should be able to sit down and discuss their differences calmly. It made him angrier when I didn't come down to his level. Had I gone down there with him, I would have been allowing the drama to carry on. Today, we still argue and he still yells, though not as bad. When he is yelling, I stare at him like he's crazy because he looks like a lunatic acting in such a way. Imagine how it would look if I acted the same. INSANE!

Drama is alive and well in my life, but it is kept at a minimum in my everyday life. The only drama I am willing to tolerate is the daily drama of being a parent of two school-aged children, and a husband who sometimes can be a handful. If someone tries to bring it in my life by stirring up mess, I cut it off by dealing with it head-on. I do not allow it to stew and go any further. I pay attention to the big-ass elephant in the room!

When my in-laws decided that they didn't like me, I did try to change their mind by spending more time with them so they could get to know me better. Whatever it is that they thought they knew about me, I know that I am a decent person, and I mean no one any harm. Like my mother says, "If I can't help you, I sure am not going to hurt you." However, they had their minds made up about me, and it seemed as though there was no turning them around.

I have always considered myself a good communicator. But as good as I thought I was, I couldn't reach his parents. They taught me a few things. They taught me that people are not always interested in knowing the truth. They only wanted to believe what they believed. They also taught me that there are some people who thrive on drama. It didn't matter what my husband or I tried, they still didn't like me being married to their son. It came down to being about what they said vs. what I said.

A cousin of my husband's came to visit us in our home for a weekend, many years ago, with her family. Shortly after the visit, my husband's father said that she told him that I had made some derogatory comments about him and his wife (that is, my in-laws). It came to a head when my husband, who had a difficult time seeing his parents for who they were, questioned me about it. I was taken aback when he asked me what I thought was a ridiculous question. I thought he knew me better than that! But I learned that he was naïve to the kind of people his parents were, because he wanted to believe what he wanted. He couldn't see the big ass elephant in the room. I saw what he was unwilling to see because of his proximity to them. In fact, I had to defend myself against an accusation that was completely false.

To this day, I am not sure that the cousin had said such a thing. For all I know it could have been completely made up to bridge a wedge between my husband and me. I was pissed at my husband for questioning me. If his cousin truly had said such a thing, his parents should have been adults enough to not let it go any further by judging me based on how I treated them; not by what they said they were told. And by the same token, my husband should have dismissed it as gossip and judged me only if he saw something in my character to suggest that I was the type of person who would do such a thing.

I went on to defend myself against their accusations. I was angry with my husband. Not because he questioned me, per se, but because he didn't use logical judgment to make a decision as to how to handle things. He allowed them to fill his head with suspicion and doubt about me. And I am the person he pledged to spend his life with, to honor. I thought that if he didn't know anything about me, he at least should have known that I would never do the things they accused me of. If he had used logic to make a decision or seen the elephant in the room, he would have caught their intentions long before it got to the point that it did.

My relationship with my in-laws suffered greatly after all of that unnecessary drama. My husband's relationship with them suffered as well. I never understood their problem with me. If I had to assume why they didn't like me, it could be because I "took" their son away from them. He was satisfied in his life with me and was no longer sharing intimate details about our life together with them. They probably felt like outsiders in their son's life and needed someone to blame. They were so busy trying to "take" him away from me that they ended up losing him. According to them, that was my fault as well.

They were, according to my husband, successful in creating drama with him and his first wife. Based on that information alone, it should have been enough for him to make an educated decision about how to handle things. But he suffered as well. He didn't want to believe that the people who gave him life would do something to cause him pain and unhappiness.

After all that was said and done, he honored the vows that we took. He honored me by not having a relationship with me that was based on rumors and gossip. But they took it to mean that he chose me over them, as he should have; I am his wife! Even if he chose me over them, what is wrong with that as long as my intentions are good by him? It's a shame really. They cheated themselves, at the time, out of having an adult relationship with their son, in addition to gaining a daughter.

Self-Esteem

20

Why is it that so many of us women have such low self-esteem? Is it because of the media? Every day, we hear and see how we're supposed to look and dress to be acceptable. The women seen on television and in magazines can look the way they do because they spend thousands of dollars and man-hours to achieve it. That is part of the problem. However, the other part of the problem is our legacy. In a relationship, much of its success or failure can depend on the woman. Yet, we let others define the relationship, whether it is our children, employers, friends, or our men.

I wrote earlier about how a woman sets the general tone of relationships. Because we give over much of our power, especially to the man in our lives, we allow him to define the relationship because we don't recognize our own power! And why don't we know our own power? We can go back again to our upbringing. But when are we going to stop blaming our past and change our future? So much of our self-worth depends on other people's opinions of us. I can tell you that, honestly, aside from my children and family, I care little for what people think of me or what think they know of me, because I know who I am. That may sound arrogant and I am not arrogant, just self-assured. It's taken many years of soul-searching, some disappointments and heartbreak to achieve it.

Imagine being in a relationship with a man for many years, and after all of those years, he has decided that the relationship is no longer working for him. There could be many reasons for it, but let's just say that he's not specific about any of them. And the way he explains it is the same as after years of having that black suit in his closet, he just up and decides that he wants something different, and the style hasn't changed that much.

Now your feelings are wounded, to say the least. You start to question your self-worth, because you will critique yourself by saying, "What's wrong with me?" This, however, has nothing to do with you. Remember, earlier I wrote about the many reasons why you have a man in your life, and one was because he has nothing better to do. This is an example of one of those reasons. Certain men are only in a relationship until the next best thing comes along. He may have been biding his time until something or someone else (better, he thinks) comes along.

This is a truth that is not always easy to face. When things were going downhill between Lover Boy and me, I confided in a more mature co-worker, just to gain a different perspective. I was still searching for a reason as to why he no longer wanted me. She told me what I didn't want to hear. She basically said that I was old news and he wanted something new! Ooh, I was pissed at her! But guess what, she was right!

Having a great sense of self can sometimes be intimidating to others. If a woman is attractive and she knows it, this can be perceived as arrogance. But if she is attractive and she doesn't see herself that way, then she has self-esteem issues. I suppose if you think you're cute and you're not, then you're just confused! But, what's wrong with a person thinking they are something special; whether they are or not? It just means they think enough of themselves to have a positive opinion of their own person.

I had someone tell me a story about how her niece grew up

looking like a boy. Her hair was short (in that it didn't seem to want to grow) and she was shapeless as a pubescent. She told me how she explained to her niece not to worry, that one day she'd change and have beautiful, long, flowing hair. Well, eventually, she did just that. She told her niece, "You see, I told you that you'd grow up to be beautiful with long hair one day!"

I would have liked to have heard her say to her niece that she was beautiful just the way she was while giving her something to look forward to! Her comment speaks volumes for how it is that we obtain bits and pieces of information that influence our self-esteem. I would never tell a young girl that she is not beautiful as she is! But this woman felt good about the comment that she made to her niece. Not because she was right, because the girl's hair grew like she had said it would. But because she thought that she had given her niece hope when it came to something superficial! What happened to making our children feel good about who they are, in the skin that they are in?

Sometime after the birth of my first child, when I was at my heaviest, weighing 270 pounds, I was not unhappy with who I was. I was unhappy with how big I was. I realized in the time it took for me to be that size, not one day passed that I didn't think about my size, or the choices that I made to keep myself at that size. The hardest thing about it was the feeling of being out of control. It was a feeling that begot another.

I had been on several job interviews for positions the requirements of which meant being out in the public dealing with people regularly. When I'd come in for the interview, I could immediately tell that I was not what they imagined I'd be, or what they wanted. I was angry at a world of people who would judge me based solely on how I looked. They judged my book (me) by its cover. It worked heavily on my self-esteem. They didn't try to get to know how good I could be for the job! However, at the time I didn't recognize it as affecting my self-esteem because I used my weight as a shield, or as an excuse for not having the life I wanted or deserved. I became a victim of my own doing, by not accepting the truth about myself; that I was not living the life I intended.

Self-esteem issues are not only about how we look. They are also about self-limitations. I could have easily used my weight as an excuse for not being able to do more or have better for the rest of my life. Losing the weight wasn't necessarily the hard part. The hard part was being honest with myself about the fact I needed to lose it. I felt limited out of fear that I wouldn't be able to accomplish it, and because I didn't know how I was going to do it. Don't get me wrong; it was very difficult, but seeing the pounds melt from my body gave me renewed confidence in my ability to do more, and try more.

My oldest sister, who has suffered from many forms of anxiety, didn't learn how to drive until she was probably about 35 years old. It shows courage, in the face of fear, to go on and do something that is challenging. I have a friend who is about the same age as my sister was when she learned to drive, and she is also in the process of learning to drive herself. They both should be commended for having the fortitude to do something that will ultimately give them the courage to do other things that they thought were outside of their reach.

Self-esteem is also about self-respect. Anyone who would allow another person to knowingly take advantage of them will suffer the consequences of their choice. Not that we haven't all been there, because it is a learning process. But to remain in that same space is detrimental to the soul!

When I was in college, I dated (well, we really didn't date, we just had sex) this cute guy. When I say he was cute, I mean that he was gorgeous! We were simply having fun, or so I thought. It was fun until he came to me one day asking me to secure a quick student loan for him. I don't remember him ever mentioning anything about paying it back either. I never had expectations of our relationship beyond what it was, so I realized that he was a user. Most likely, he thought his good looks would get him what he wanted, as I am sure they had in the past. He probably also thought that because I was a big girl, and therefore supposedly desperate for male attention, it would make it easier to get what he wanted. But the only thing it got him was some pussy, and that was okay, because it was all I planned on giving to him.

This may sound cliché, but respect, as I'm sure you've heard, is something that is earned, not demanded or paid for. Respect is also not automatic. If you want it, you have to live it. Remember the Golden Rule: "Do unto others as you would *have* others do unto you." It is not: do unto others *as* others do unto you! My in-laws may have not been God-like in their relationship with me, but to take out revenge on them goes not only against the Golden Rule, but ultimately against God's law.

I live every day knowing that I did nothing to have caused any of the resentment they felt toward me. I had nothing to prove by retaliating and doing to them what they did to me, because I know who I am. It has taken many years, but the respect that my father-in-law (my mother-in-law is no longer with us) now has for me comes from the fact that I treat him no differently than if he had never done what he did. You don't have to love a person to respect them and you don't have to like a person to love them. You don't even have to like a person to respect them. One thing has absolutely nothing to do with the other.

I'm truly grateful to say that I have love in my life, but above all, I have respect. Respect by definition is having consideration, regard, honor and esteem for self and others. It is impossible to have respect for self and not others, or vice versa. That is not respect. That is a power play to show who has the most power in the relationship.

It is nothing new that I have been disrespected in relationships. But to continue a relationship that is based on my being disregarded is to dishonor myself. So then it becomes about what I have become because of what happened to me, rather than what happened to me! That's deep!

It was not enough that I found out that I was sharing Lover Boy with another woman. I also had to find out that I had been sharing him with her for more than a minute; that my friends had seen him out with her on more than one occasion. To allow myself to continue in a relationship with him after the many revelations would have meant to dishonor myself. Not only that, but to go on in a relationship where someone other than myself is aware of my being disrespected is unacceptable to me. By walking away from the relationship it became a situation that happened to me rather than what I decided to become, disrespected!

Desiderata

Desiderata are plural for *desideratum*. It means "things that are needed and desired." Max Ehrmann wrote my favorite poem during the first quarter of the twentieth century. There are many people struggling in life because they can't quite find their way or because they lack direction. This poem could offer respite to someone struggling to find peace in their life. For me, it represents a beautiful way to peacefully experience life.

Were it not for copyright infringement laws, conflicting court judgments, and circumstances which have created a good dose of mystery as to whether or not this poem is in the public domain, I definitely would have included it in this book. It can however, be searched on the Internet using the keyword: Desiderata. Hopefully, you will find it as undeniably truthful as I have.

Get It
Together

Moving On   22

The theory that the way to get over a man is with a new one is
not true. It may be true if the relationship was a casual affair.
That would mean that there was no real investment of feelings on
either part. But if the relationship was one with genuine feelings
on your part, then it would not be in your best interest to get
involved with another person too soon.

There are steps that should be taken to get past a breakup. The
first step is to heal. It is unfortunate, but the only way to heal
from a breakup is to experience the pain of it all, and it can only
be done by experiencing each stage of grief. (In no particular order,
the stages of grief are: anger, denial, bargaining, depression, and
acceptance. Dr. Elisabeth Kübler-Ross identified those five stages
to describe each step by which people process grief or tragedy.)
Jumping into a relationship quickly after one has ended will
sabotage your ability to heal from the breakup. This is that time
I spoke of earlier—the time necessary to get to know who you
are. Because as I asked earlier, how can you know who you are if
you've never been alone? If what you are running from are the
depressing and hurtful feelings that you're experiencing, you
may as well run all of your life. Life is full of ups and downs and
this will be just one of those times. If every time you experience
loss, disappointment or sadness and you move on, without so
much as a whimper, you will be cheating yourself from the full

benefit of healing. Healing is the first line of defense to moving on.

It's okay to be sad and hurt. It's even okay to wallow in your sadness, just not forever! With all of the tears that you're shedding, be sure that you know what it is that you're crying over. Are you crying over the thought of being alone, because you love him and you thought that he loved you, too? Or is it because he has become a habit that you're having a difficult time breaking? It doesn't matter what the answer is. Just like taking a test, use your power of reasoning (the process of elimination) to come up with an answer by seeing it for what it is. Once you get past all the sorrow, you may find out that he was never worth your tears. Depending on how decent of a man he was will depend on how he ended it. Because a real man does not achieve gratification from causing you pain.

If you've shared your heartbreak with others, you will no doubt have them trying to help you by telling you how you should deal with it. But whatever you do, take your time deciding. It's very important that you say what you mean, and mean what you say. If you don't, your bluff will be called and you'll be found out as a person not of your word and therefore easily taken advantage of. Then, you'll walk around for the rest of your life being afraid to let people in for fear of being hurt again.

After all of the sadness and pain begin to fade away; you'll probably start to feel pissed off at the person who has left you broken-hearted. This is a healthy phase. Just don't take it to the extreme and try to get your own kind of justice. Believe me when I say, they will get theirs! Whether you give it to them or not, something or someone will beat you to the punch. Better them than you. You wouldn't want to jeopardize your future because of a temporary lapse of sanity! This is the time when it's important to be the grownup.

Your anger may come from your not ever having the opportunity to get closure because you weren't able to express to the other party how it is they made you feel. When someone hurts you, they don't know your pain. They don't care! It was never about you; it was always about them and what they wanted. That's why it is so important that you take your time to heal. Be in the moment of the pain; deal with it so that you can provide your own sense of closure. Not giving you that sense of closure is their way of maintaining control! It is an awful shame when someone takes their affection away without allowing you a choice in the matter.

When Lover Boy broke my heart, I was in the most incredible amount of pain I could have ever imagined. I had never been so hurt in all of my life. The pain of losing him felt worse than the pain of losing someone to death. I know it sounds pitiful, but I *was* pitiful! I remember looking up at the sky during one of my crying spells, and feeling sad because I longed for his presence: I knew he was inhaling the same air that I breathed, just from somewhere else, not with me.

When we first broke up, I didn't have any feelings of hurting myself; I was just sad. I always knew that another day would come and that it would be better than the day before. I counted on it. I found something to spend my time doing: putting puzzles together. Instead of concentrating on him, I concentrated on where that single, tiny, puzzle piece would be placed in a 1,500-piece puzzle board. I put them together, glued them and had them framed for wall art. I had to. I didn't want to spend my time getting sucked into a routine of being sad all of the time, crying over him. I didn't deserve to let myself go by the wayside because he did wrong by me. If anyone deserved that outcome, it was he! By the way, this was the one time I wished I had a father. Had I had one, he surely would have sought him out and kicked his ass!

I couldn't understand why I was so devastated over the breakup. It wasn't like we had children together, or had been together for years and years and years (I have mentioned earlier that the relationship was just shy of one year). The way I carried on, you would have thought that I had spent the last ten years of my life with him! When I started on my journey to get past the breakup, it was all about trying to prove something to him. The best revenge is to live well. As the process went along, I realized that it was not him that I needed to prove anything to; I had to prove it all to myself! First and foremost, I started to open myself up again to the friends who I had been either too embarrassed or too exhausted to talk to. I got involved in doing new things and meeting new people. By the time I saw him again, I was feeling fine and looking well, and he was the same. The difference was that I no longer desired him, and he was someone else's problem!

The second step necessary for surviving a breakup is to forgive yourself for the mistakes that you may have made, whether you were the reason for the breakup or because you chose the wrong man to have a relationship with. You wouldn't be the first woman to choose the wrong man for the wrong reason. There are so many such reasons; he had potential, a good job, he was good-looking, made good love to you, or you didn't know that he was crazy and you should have known better! When you allow yourself to see the big-ass elephant sitting in the room from the beginning, you have a better chance of getting out before too much time and feelings have been invested into such a person.

The third step is to spend time with yourself to rediscover what is important to you. Rather than obsessing over what you don't have, be grateful for what you do! My blessing, for example, was that I didn't marry a man who was capable of hurting me so badly. There are many women out there wishing for the companionship of a man, and that's okay. But they still have to find one that's worth their time! In the meantime, they should be spending their time with the people they are already connected with or reconnect with the ones that they've not seen in a while.

We have to be able to acknowledge that we chose the wrong person. We try so hard to prove to the world that our man is perfect and he is the best thing that ever happened to us. However, if he were perfect, or at least as close as one can get to perfection in the real world, we wouldn't have to try so hard for others to notice it. We then try to protect his image because we know that *we* are judged by the company we keep. If he is not "Mr. Wonderful," it is important to realize that it's okay. It's not your fault. Whatever he is, let him be. If he's a liar, he's a liar. If he's a whore, he's a whore. If he's an asshole, he's an asshole. If it quacks like a duck... Let it be whatever it is and deal with it! See the big-ass elephant sitting in the middle of the floor. Being in denial will only hurt *you* in the end.

Ladies, what is the worst that could happen if you decided to question or challenge the negativity going on in your relationship? Depending on the type of man you have in your life and the dynamics of that relationship, the situation will determine his response. If the worst he does is to decide that *he* will leave and not tolerate your behavior (derived from your self-awareness), then he leaves! Wouldn't that tell you what kind of man he is, or that he is not committed to the relationship or you? And isn't that what you really want to know? Or do you just want to know that you have a man around, which is not very much at all? It's much better to know early on what you are dealing with rather than spending your precious time on someone who means you no good!

Forgiveness

Forgiveness

23

I'm sure you've heard so many times before how important it is to forgive. Even the worst offenses against a person need to be forgiven. I don't mean to say you should forgive and forget. Forgetting is like saying something never happened. I am a firm believer in remembering the ugly side of the past in order to not have it repeated in the future. Forgiving is necessary because when you hold on to the negative feelings of a past hurt or injustice, you block your ability to move forward in your life with all of the possibilities of what can be.

During the last two months of my pregnancy, with my firstborn, my husband's relationship with his parents, especially his father, became exceptionally tense. He hid many conversations between himself and his family from me. He says it was because he didn't want to stress me out. The final fallout came on the day when my child was born. He called his parents to make them aware of the birth of their grandchild. According to my husband, he was speaking to his mother on the phone and the conversation was going quite well, considering the situation. But then his father walked into the room and asked who was on the phone. When he found out it was his son calling about the birth of his new grandchild, *HE HUNG UP THE PHONE IN MY HUSBAND'S FACE!!!*

I wish I could say that my husband was devastated, and maybe he would have been, but considering what happened later on, at this time he was just moderately distressed. By the time our baby was about six months old, I encouraged my husband to travel back to our hometown and have a sit-down with his family to try and resolve the issues that were keeping them apart. We did it, and it didn't go so well. To talk about exactly what happened would be another chapter or book!

Believe me, it was a lot of yelling, name-calling, finger-pointing, neck-gyrating, and everyone trying to be right. I was so hurt for my husband. He loved his family to a fault. In fact, until this point in his life, he had never even suffered the trauma of being heart-broken, not even by a woman. So this experience was new for him. I ended up leaving the house and asked him to call me when he was ready to leave. I no longer wanted to be a party to the drama; it was too much!

When I returned to pick him up, I brought my baby so they could see her in person. In my mind, it would be the only time they would get the chance to see or hold her. That was how bad it went. His mother held her, but his father looked at her with an attempted smile. How horrifying! Children are a gift from God. With the many responsibilities that parents are charged with, one is to keep their children safe while providing a loving environment. And with that, they can hopefully grow to be well-adjusted, caring adults. I didn't want her around people who couldn't care less that she even existed.

Well, my husband made the decision to continue to have a part in his parents' life. I supported him in that, but I couldn't be bothered. They were downright mean and nasty to me and I didn't have to deal with it because they were not my parents. But the drama continued to unfold; if I didn't mention it before, let me now…

It so happened that we went back home a couple of months

later. He swung by their house to visit them without me, or our child (I had already told him that she would never return to that home and he accepted my decision.)

A few weeks later (I will never forget it; it was the Friday prior to Labor Day 1998), we went to the mailbox to pick up the mail, on our way up the street to pick up our daughter from the baby-sitter who lived in our subdivision. I was pushing the stroller and my husband was going through the mail when he saw an envelope addressed to him in his father's handwriting. He opened it. Inside, there were pictures of our beautiful baby girl (taken at three months old) that had been sent to his parents before the fight, a few months back. Horror of horrors, they were scribbled on with a marker and cut into several small pieces. Now he was devastated!

Why did his father do it? I believe that it was to prove a point (what exactly that point was, I never knew), or to stick it to him. I suspect the latter. I've seen his parents in action and how they use emotional blackmail to get what they want from their children. I believe that when his parents could not get from him what they wanted (for him to obey them as he did as a child), his father resorted to the next best thing in his mind: "stick it to him where it hurts." And it did. It hurt my husband unspeakably (all it did to me was piss me off, more!) It didn't hurt because of the pictures being torn, but because our daughter was innocent in all of this mess. And it was despicable that his father would do something as awful as that (and that his mother allowed it to happen).

Now that was nine years ago. We worked really hard on ourselves to not become hardened and we were able to eventually forgive them for what they had done. But when I tell you that I have not forgotten, believe that! I keep those slashed pictures in my home as a reminder of what was done. It reminds me of the kind of parent I want to be.

Had I held on to those feelings of anger and resentment, I would have given over my ability to move forward. Forgiving them was not about their saying to us, "We're sorry." It was also not about us forgetting what was done. (Because forgetting, like I said before, is like saying it never happened. As parents, we owe it to our children not to forget.) Not forgiving, however, causes you to become a victim of circumstance or someone else's choosing. It just holds you back!

My little sister made a mistake. She said something to a family member that was not well received. I don't think that what she said was wrong; it was just said at the wrong time. She has apologized for it on several occasions with a phone call. It has been over six months and that person has yet to return a single call. Why hasn't she returned her call? Is it because she is embarrassed because she knows my sister was right? Or is it because she *doesn't* want to forgive her?

It takes a big person to say they are sorry. It takes an even bigger person to forgive! It is a blessing to have someone in our life that will tell us something for our own good. It is also a blessing that even if they were wrong, they had courage enough to say, "I'm sorry."

What Do You Expect?

24

What do you expect? (You expect nothing, you get nothing!) It is probably a question you seldom ask yourself, but it should be something you ask yourself every time you become involved in a relationship. Or in general if the outcome has not only to do with your personal participation, but with the involvement of a loved one, your money, time, and things, etc. We become so involved and invested in a relationship right out of the gate and never take the time to ask ourselves what we expect from that relationship.

Just as you should have an expectation of everything you become involved in, others should have an expectation of you. You expect an incentive for being a good employee: a raise. You expect that if you paid good money for a product, you should get your money's worth. When you don't get what you expect, hopefully you will do something about it. Your something about it could be as simple as finding a new job, returning your product for either a refund or a new and improved model, or simply learning from the experience so as to not repeat it.

In a relationship, if you don't get what you expect, why do you stay? If you expect nothing, you get nothing. That includes you! Do you ever wonder what is expected of you? As an employee, if you've not done what your employer expects of you, then you should expect to either be reprimanded or terminated, right? It is the same in any relationship.

A relationship is a relationship, whether it is husband and wife, parent and child, siblings, employee to employer, friend-to-friend, neighbor-to-neighbor, etc.; some may not be equal in the hierarchy, but they are all similar conceptually. When you don't get what you expect, in a relationship, it is because of several reasons. For example, it could be because what you expect is no longer of importance. You did not clearly communicate to that other entity what you could bring to the table. Or you didn't communicate, clearly, what you wanted or needed from the relationship, and that goes all the way back to communication.

One day, I was watching *The View* and in this particular episode, there was a comedienne as the guest co-host. She basically made the comment that if her husband cheated on her, it wouldn't be a deal breaker. She said that she would want him to be honest so that they could work through it! Is that what she expects? What is she saying; that a lie about his fidelity is the deal breaker? Maybe. But my concern is that it sounded a lot like her not having faith in him to do the right thing. It also sounded like her not having faith in herself because she fears she may not be able to hold him accountable for the kind of relationship she wants with him.

Does she expect him to cheat on her or does she want to prepare herself for being possibly cheated on so as not to be devastated? The comment speaks volumes for the current state of relationships. If she expects to be cheated on, then she expects less than what she deserves, so why get married? We live in such a "micro-waveable" society, everything is disposable, and nothing means anything anymore. We have become so desensitized to everything. Nothing is sacred, not even the institution of marriage.

Aside from expecting less than what we deserve, some of us women expect a fairy tale life with a man, which is impossible. It is possible to have a perfectly, imperfect relationship, but not a fairy tale. Just give that prince enough time to turn into a frog, trust me, his warts will eventually start to show!

Expecting a fairy tale is like expecting perfection. No such thing exists. You can pretend that it is a fairy tale, but everyone around you, including you, will know the real deal! I asked a young lady who was newly married to let me know how she was doing. Meaning how was she adjusting to married life. She said she was having fun! I thought, "Shit, really. FUN?!"

Wow, I have never heard marriage being described as fun. It can be entertaining, especially when kids are involved. It can be stressful, like a roller coaster, or heartbreaking, depending on the circumstances. But, fun? She was still in the newlywed stage; I expect that once that phase was over, it was no longer fun. I love my husband, and I know that he loves me. But let me tell you, he gives me hell, and I give him the blues. It may not be all of what I expected, but it is a reality that I can live with.

My husband thought that he could be married to me and just get by. When you're in school trying to make the grades, sometimes it can become overwhelming, so you'll do just enough to get by. You may want to make an A or a B, but you become satisfied with earning a C. Well, at one point, my husband treated the relationship he has with our children and me as though his grade only had to be a C. Not good enough!

He said that, after a day's work, he'd be too tired to come home and get involved with something else. What the hell! It didn't matter how much I had been involved with something, or how tired I was. I would think to myself, does he hear what he is saying to me? Does he understand the words that are coming out of his mouth?

He didn't understand what he was saying. He thought he was just saying, "I'm tired." But what I heard him saying was, "I'm tired. *You* can do whatever it is that needs to be done. Or whatever it is that needs to be done is not important." And of course, if it's not important to him, then it's not important at all!

I told him to remember that he gets paid in money for the job he has outside of the home. I also told him that he needed to realize that the children and I are a job just like the one that he gets paid money for. I explained to him what he already knew. His boss has an expectation that he would fulfill his job duties, and one of the consequences of not performing those duties could cause him to hear the words, "You're fired!"

Although my husband is not paid in money for the work he puts in for being a husband and a father, his reward is having healthy, beautiful, and smart children who love and adore him. He also has a woman who, when she's feeling satisfied in her life with him, because he knows what is expected of him, is able to make him feel like the king that he deserves to be!

Who Are You?

25

With all of life's expectations, what do you expect from yourself? As I just previously mentioned, we have many expectations of the people in our lives, but rarely do we think that those same people may have expectations of us as we should, ultimately, have of ourselves. Who exactly are you? If someone asked you that question, how would you answer? Or better yet, would you be able to answer? I am not talking about your wardrobe, where and how you live, how beautiful you are, but about what is important to you! Outside of my children, my greatest accomplishment is me: being who I am, who I chose to be. Being comfortable in my own skin, with my own bills and having my own collection of problems.

I wrote earlier about how dysfunction in men manifests itself. They become liars, cheaters, users, and abusers. What about women? We become jealous, catty, judgmental, bitter and revenge seekers. Basically, we cry, bitch and moan.

It is unfortunate that if you are a strong woman, generally speaking, your strength could no doubt be perceived as bitchy. I've witnessed firsthand female leaders, who expected a lot from the people they employ, earn the moniker of "bitch." If a man were to demand the same thing with the same set of conditions, he would be labeled "good at what he does." It sucks that there is still a double standard that exists. That a woman can't be good at what she does, even when she expects a lot from the people around her, including herself. I assume it could be because of the perception others have of us; that because we are emotionally involved in things, we crack under pressure. How can that be true if a woman is the backbone of her family? The man may be the head of the household, and often times that can be debated, but we are the true backbone of the family. We make *it* happen for everyone around us, including ourselves.

We become jealous, catty, judgmental, bitter, and revenge seekers when we don't get what we want. I don't mind being called a bitch if the shoe fits, but I mind anyone knowing that I am any of the other aforementioned. I wrote the word "knowing" because people are going to think and say what they want to; you have no control over it. But, they also know the truth, whether or not they acknowledge it!

If I am not living the life that I want or deserve, first of all, I know that I am ultimately responsible for it. Second, anything else would suggest that I have allowed myself to surrender to a life that someone or something else has conjured up for me. I see, on a daily basis, women not living their life to its fullest potential because they give in to the life that they are presently living by being what others want them to be.

If you found out that your man was cheating, what would you do? Would you take a bat to his automobile or slash his tires? All in the hope that he remembers the consequences of his actions before he does it again?

If we are to be changed by our experiences, who in this situation is supposed to be the one who's changed: the one who has cheated or the one who slashed the tires? A woman who would allow herself to continue in the same situation over and over again still hasn't learned from the first time and neither has he. A woman such as this has allowed herself to become a woman that's cheated on, and therefore is cheating herself by surrendering to a life that is not of her choosing.

Who are you and what do you want for yourself? If you want a friend, be a friend. If you want a good husband, be a good wife. If you want respect, be respectful. If you want love, show love. Remember the principle of reciprocity. It's like a boomerang. If you throw it out there in the world, it will come back to you. If it doesn't, find someone else to throw it to! But above all, remember that whatever it is that you want from someone, be *it* to yourself.

Who I am and what I am did not come out of a cereal box. I didn't just wake up one day and decided on the life I wanted and *poof*, there it was. It also didn't happen just because I said I wanted it. About two years after I had gotten married, I remember my mother saying to me that she had wondered in the past what kind of woman I would become once I was married. She went on to say that she was pleased to know the woman I had become because she knows how women can lose themselves in a marriage.

A few months after my husband and I were married, I told him that I was still waiting to feel different. I thought marriage was supposed to change me. It was like I was waiting to experience a symphony or a rainbow to symbolize my completion as a person in the marriage! I finally realized that it wasn't going to happen, because I was the same person and because maybe I was fine the way I was. We were just two people that had been joined together in marriage. That's it! Nothing grand, just two people joined together.

Once I realized that, my life was simpler to manage. I understood that I could be my own person in the marriage. It went okay for a minute, but soon my husband began to become distant and angry every time my family would come around, especially my mother. It was because he knew that I loved her just as much as I loved him, if not more! I had to get him to see that I had enough love for him and my family to go around and that there was no competition. Since that time they've come to really know one another. My husband loves my mother like the mother he has come to wish he had. And my mother loves my husband like another son. Remember, earlier I said that you can't choose the family that you were born into, but you can make a better choice when it comes to the people you decide to be a part of your life, including the person you decide to spend the rest of your life with.

I realize that if I had married a different man, I could have become a different woman. In the beginning of my marriage, if my husband were the cheating type, it could have potentially changed who I became. I probably would have taken that luggage out of the foyer and brought it into the middle of our relationship. I am hopeful, though, that I would have made the decision to see it as his mistake for doing it to me, or my mistake for allowing it to continue.

I can see why women lose themselves in relationships. It became evident during the time when I was dealing with my husband and his attitude toward my family. It became exhausting and it could have been easier to just let him have what he wanted. He would be nitpicky and go on and on complaining about nothing. But in my eyes, that's like letting someone choose what I am going to wear, who my friends are going to be, what I can eat, where I can go, if I can go; you get my drift!

The greatest freedom we have is freedom of choice. I love my husband, but my freedom of choice is more important to me. My husband knows that I can love him and still be my own person. One thing has nothing to do with the other. Who I am requires effort. It is the greatest gift I have given to myself…better than the first designer bag I ever bought for myself! We are all a work in progress. Learn not just from your own experiences, but the experiences of others. The day that any of us get to a point where we can't learn from someone or something is a sad day, and is a day on which humility can be replaced with arrogance and stupidity.

Who's the Man?

26

I asked you, who are you? Now I am asking you: do you know what kind of man your man is? Or better yet, who is the man in the relationship? Is your man a liar, user, cheater or abuser? You know! If you don't know, you had better open your eyes to see the big ass elephant sitting in the room. It's possible that he may be none of those things but whatever the case, you need to know who he is. When you are clear about what kind of people you are dealing with, it will be easier to know their intentions.

I was watching *Judge Judy* one day and saw yet another woman allowing herself to be taken advantage of by a man (who was younger by half her age). She had purchased him a car. He eventually broke it off with her and he traded the car in for a new and improved model, no pun intended. He was relatively good-looking. I suspect he thought his good looks would get him what he wanted.

There used to be a time, back in the day, that when a man liked a woman, he would woo her. Now the women are doing the wooing. I have had many conversations with my mother and she has told me how men used to be. Men used to be the one to approach the woman, buy her a drink, a meal, etc. They used to be the breadwinner. They were simply a man's man.

Back in the day, and before then, men had to be men. The only thing a woman was good for was cooking, cleaning and making babies. Women did not have choices. We have accomplished so much since that time and have taken advantage of our accomplishments. It was unheard of then to see a woman be the CEO of a major corporation. It was also unheard of for a woman to be asking a man out on a date. Today, not only are we asking them out, we are paying for it! Personally, I do not mind asserting myself by letting a man know how I feel about him. But to buy his meal, affection or time is out of the question!

A long time ago, I could feel things starting to change between Lover Boy and me. He would say that everything was okay when I would ask, but I could feel the distance between us. And everything I did got on his nerves. I wanted nothing more than to please him and for him to be happy. Because I was happy when he was happy! Yuck!

His credit was not the best, so I agreed to finance a big-screen TV for him because it was what he wanted. I thought as long as he was happy, then we would be together, and therefore I would be happy. *Fortunately* for me, less than two months after he'd gotten what he wanted, he broke it to me that we needed to spend some time apart. I was heartbroken. Why I was so devastated? He had been showing me signs all along that my days with him were numbered. I didn't want to see the big-ass elephant. I thought that if I did this thing for him, it would make things different between us, and that he'd feel satisfied being in the relationship with me. All I did was simply prolong the inevitable. It didn't matter how I tried to "buy" his love, he still went on to someone else. I didn't want to see it. Anyway, I got stuck paying the bill. I learned my lesson. Considering how it could have ended had I stayed with him, I got off cheap and easy!

A real man would have never asked for such a thing. A real man would be satisfied with what he has, until he could afford to pay for his wants. A real woman would not feel she has to pay for the affection from a man, as I did. I didn't do it for him out of fear of being alone. I did it because I *loved* him.

Chivalry is dead! It is sad but true. What has happened to men opening the door for women? And when was the last time a man held a door open for you? I can't tell you the countless times that a man has allowed a door to close in my face, including my own husband (because he wasn't paying attention). Hell, I've even stood outside the passenger car door just waiting on him to unlock it, and he was already sitting in the car on the driver's side with the engine on!

Once I was at a carnival, and lost control of the foam football I threw in the wrong direction (that's no surprise). It was rolling on the ground toward a young man, who stopped it with his foot, and used the same foot to push it back toward my direction. I was standing right next to him by this time but he didn't even bend over to give it to me! I'm sure he thought that what he did was acceptable.

Another time, I was walking down a long hallway. When I got to the doors (they were swinging doors with glass in the middle so that you can see down the hallway), there was a man on the other side. He waited until I was close and opened the door for me! I could have sworn I heard "fireworks!" He even asked me, "Were you surprised that I opened the door for you?" He must have seen the "look of awe" on my face. He also said, "That's what men are supposed to do. When he sees a woman, he is to stop and allow her to go first." He was an older gentleman and obviously thought I needed to be enlightened. He also said that women are supposed to wait for the man to do it! But what he doesn't realize is that had it been another man I was waiting on to open the door for me, I'd still be standing in the same spot!

What has happened to chivalry? One thing I know has happened to it is a woman's success. Let me stop to explain what I mean. With all of the professional success, we have failed in our personal lives. We have allowed the men to become a shadow of their predecessors by making things easier for them.

There are many very successful men. But that is nothing new, because it's a man world. However, with all of women's successes, it has become more difficult to find a man who is able to be with a truly accomplished woman. He either feels intimidated by her success or he tries to use it for his own personal gain. If she gets involved with someone who is in it only for what he can get out of it, she has allowed herself to settle for less. She becomes the breadwinner of the relationship, and therefore his role has been redefined. And that's okay. There are many women who are the breadwinners of their families. It works for them, because the husbands, in turn, do their part in the family unit. It becomes a team effort.

Women have become so involved in their own personal involvements that they have lost sight of the whole picture. I strongly believe that a woman can have a successful career, as well as success in her personal life. If we apply the same principles to having a successful career as we would with the man in our life, we could have both.

My husband would come home from a hard day's work and crash, despite the fact that there would be household things that needed to be done. He would go on to say how hard *his* day was. As though what my day was like didn't matter. As I have already said, I remember telling him in so many words that we, the kids and I, were a job no less than the one he gets paid for. The result in both is that he could get fired. I know that this comment seems harsh on paper, but it needed to be said. I have no intention of being in a relationship with a husband who doesn't know what is expected of him. I have, in the past, done twice as much household work than my husband will ever know. When he does it, he wants recognition for it. When I do it, it's just what I am supposed to do.

When a man becomes successful, just turn on the television and you will see it. He marries a woman that is half his age, twice as beautiful and possibly half his size. Women that are just as successful may not be able to find their match, because her equivalent has chosen someone that is *not* his match! If she is not able to find the man just for her, then she is either choosing not to marry, or choosing the wrong man for the wrong reason.

This may be a bold statement, but I am going to say it anyway. We have crippled our men. We have taken away their ability to be a man. We have made it way too easy for them. We are settling for less and not holding them accountable for how they treat us.

Early in my marriage, my husband wanted a part-time job so that we could get ahead with our bills. I didn't want him to get another job because that would have meant less time he'd spend with me! I remember having that conversation with my mother and she said to me, "Baby, you don't make it easy for no man, I don't care if he is your husband!" That was a big *Hmm* moment for me. I thought all I was doing was showing him how much I loved him. But my mother painted a different picture for me. I was telling him that making provisions for us, which was a good decision on his part, should take a back seat to my desires. In essence, I tried to discourage his ability to do the right thing for our family and ultimately himself, to be a man!

It must be nice being a man in a world of women. How wonderful it must be to live your life freely and openly without fear of guilt or retribution for any of your wrongdoings. Many men live this life, all because their women allow them to hide behind them.

My husband and I were married less than a year when we traveled back to our hometown and made a visit to see his best friend's parents. This was their first time meeting me. We were all standing outside on the porch and the front yard talking. Sometime while talking, the conversation was taken inside of their house. Somehow I was left outside, alone. Now, my husband wasn't the one to come back outside to reclaim me. It was his friend's mother. She apologized for leaving me outside and I told her it was no problem and that I was used to it! If looks could kill! By the time I made my comment, he had come outside, just after her. He gave me a look like he could just strangle me. He was upset about what I had said because it did not put him in the best light. I can guarantee you that he only came outside because she made a comment like, "Where's your wife?"—and not because he noticed that I was not in the room! I was pissed off because it wasn't the first time he has disregarded me in the presence of other people.

My husband, just as many men, wants to be perceived as the perfect husband or mate. He is a good person, but as a husband, sometimes he fall short. He thinks his only contribution to me, besides earning a living, is being the kind of husband that doesn't cheat on me or party constantly. But I have to remind him that I am not to be taken for granted. I will not allow his bad behavior to remain in the dark, just so that he can look like some knight-in-shining-armor. And then I'd look like an idiot for trying to pretend to have something I don't have: the perfect husband!

Man Up

27

Even though some men have bad habits, women could learn a few things from men in one way: they don't take *everything* personally. Not only do we women take many things personally, we also have a tendency of putting everyone's needs and feelings in front of our own, and that needs to stop. We can't be anything and everything to everybody; we have to be everything to ourselves.

My husband would do something knowing full well that when he did it, I wouldn't like it. Now I ask you, knowing the difference between being stupid or ignorant, which of the two was he being? I'll let you answer that. Anyway, when he had done it, and after I would make a gesture to signify my disapproval or disappointment, he would apologize for it, ask me to forgive him, and then ask for a kiss! I would look at him like he had lost his mind.

What did he think I was, an inanimate object, nobody that required any consideration or forethought? I would be an afterthought! It was as though he thought he could snap his fingers, and *poof*, it's over (whatever he had done and my pissed-offedness toward him). He would want things to go back to exactly the way they were between us just before he had done what he had done.

My husband has, from the beginning, thought that what I needed to do was just adjust to his "bad behavior" and get used to it. I know it, because he said so (another ditch that he dug for himself). Like I've said before, he thought that all he needed to do to be in a relationship was be a warm body. But I always needed more than that from him; I wouldn't have married him unless I thought he could give me more. And I wouldn't have stayed married to him if he hadn't given it to me!

When I get mad, I have a tendency of not letting go. It takes more than a minute to remove the image of what has been done to me out of my mind. It is my one and only flaw!!! Ha, Ha.

Once, at my husband's family reunion celebration, we played a type of newlywed game (none of the couples participating was newly wedded.) One of the questions that were asked of the men was: *what kind of animal do you think your wife would describe herself as?*

When we came back from being sequestered, I answered, a lion. It seemed logical to me because our high school mascot was the Mighty Lion, and there was nothing else I could think of. I thought maybe the lion matched up more to my personality than any other animal I could think of. I wouldn't have ever described myself as some kind of delicate animal like a dove. It doesn't suit me. But neither did my husband. He called me a pit bull! Everyone roared with laughter. I laughed too when I realized how he came to the conclusion. I am like a pit bull in that when I get a hold of something (in reference to my beliefs and ideals), I don't let go!

I digressed. Let me get back to not taking things personally. I do take it personally when my husband does something to disregard me. Because it *is* personal; he is my husband. If he tells me that he is going to do something, I expect him to do it. If he can't, I expect him to say that. But for him to not do as he says, and then pretend as though it didn't happen, or that I should be okay with it after the fact because he said that he was sorry, is not good enough.

When we were first married and he did something to disregard me, I would be so hurt, like a wounded deer. I have cried many nights, in my pillow, because he disregarded my feelings by saying or doing something that was completely insensitive or hurtful. But after being together for more than fifteen years, I don't go for that Pollyanna shit anymore. I am no longer the wounded animal, and not because I am capable of speaking up for myself. But because after being with him for as many years as I have been with him, he knows me better than that!

So now, when he does or says something that is hurtful or insensitive, I become an angry, pissed-off Black woman, because as I said, he knows me better than that! When it happens, I say what I have to say. I don't hold it in because I don't want to implode on myself. It is much more cathartic to share my feelings and colorful words with him.

But someone insignificant does not have the power to affect me in such a way. I work with people who just think they know me. They think they know me because they think that just because I smile a lot and say good morning, thank you and please, that somehow I am a pushover. In the few times that I have been tested, I swiftly made sure that they knew that it is not who I am!

For the most part, I get along with everyone. But I know there are some who don't particularly care for me, and I don't give a damn! I have been labeled a troublemaker on jobs of the past because I speak up for myself. I don't go to work to make friends. I go to do a job that I am paid for, and I do it well! However, it does make it easier to do a job when there is someone there that you can connect with, even if it's just during work hours. I have been fortunate enough to meet some incredible people at work who are now my friends in and outside of the job.

When I was the new kid on the block, I could sense sometimes how I was being made to feel like an outsider. It may have not been the intention, but I could feel the energy. I am not the kind of person who needs to belong to a group in order feel secure, so it wasn't hard for me to find my own way. I developed a relationship with my co-workers on my own terms.

If I had taken what I felt personally, I would have had to believe that they didn't want me there. How could that be possible when they didn't even know me? And if I were to have taken their actions toward me personally, it would have meant that I would have been able to be emotional about it. And how do I become emotional about something that was new to me? I had no time or feelings invested in it. Also, how do I take offense to something that has nothing to do with me?

If I am being made to feel like an outsider, it is because the people who are trying to make me feel insecure are the grown people with the problems, not me. I was not going to be the one sitting over in a corner feeling sorry for myself because I wanted to belong to their Club of Stupid!

Man up and put yourself first, before anyone. There are some who are now gasping just after reading that statement. Gasping because I didn't say put God first. Put God first! When you put God first, you put yourself first! When you put yourself first, you put God first! God is in each and every one of us. Because He is in us, when we take care of ourselves by trying to live right, we honor Him. We honor Him by taking care of self first. How can you care for the people who depend on you for their survival if you are not caring for yourself in the way God intended? God gives us the tools to navigate our way through life, but we don't use them!

At the risk of sounding like I am being judgmental, I am going to say something. I worked with a woman whose husband didn't work. When I say he didn't work, I mean he did nothing! Not wash a dish, keep the house clean or anything, according to her. She said that she would have to go home at the end of a workday and clean up and prepare dinner. He even had the nerve to drop her off at work and keep the car all day long. What does he need a car for during the day if he was not actively looking for a job? He probably was telling her that he was looking for a job so that he could keep the car. But I don't think it takes more than two years to need the car and still not have a job (the length of time that she and I worked together).

Sounding defeated, I heard her saying to someone in regards to her husband not having a job: "I just put it in God's hands." That's terrible! She's hiding behind God. She used Him as an excuse for not living her life the way *He* intended. Possibly because if she had allowed herself to see it for what it was, she would have been compelled to make a different decision, that is, to get rid of him! God gave her the ability, just as He did with everyone else, to make a decision on her own, but she wanted to have God be accountable for the life of her choosing! Too many people are waiting for God to fix it, but God is waiting to see what you do!

You know what you put in God's hands? When your child, heaven forbid, is ill and there is nothing you can do about it. When you have lost your job and there is not one in sight. When you need to feed your kids and you have no one to turn to or have no resources. When you need or want something, and you've done all that is humanly possible to get it. That is when you put it in God's hands.

The friendship I had that ended, I spoke of it earlier, ended because she didn't want a deeper relationship with me than what it had been. We had a superficial relationship. A deeper relationship would have meant for her to be open and honest with me. It would have primarily required that she be honest with herself, and I believe it was just not something that was possible for her at the time.

When I tried to talk about it with her, she said that we didn't need to discuss it any longer because, in her own words, "You said that it was your problem, so I'll let you handle it." She also said, "I've put it in God's hands." There it was again. Why put something in God's hands that is right in front of you to deal with! I was right there! But saying it made it easier for her to put it off on something or someone else and not take responsibility for its conclusion. If she and I are not friends anymore, it is because she didn't want to have a relationship with me the way I needed it to be. That was certainly her prerogative. But I could no longer be a friend with someone who was not willing to let me be free to be myself, as I needed to be. Because for me what was more important was being me, and not being the person she wanted me to be.

As long as I have known her, and before her, I have always been a deep thinker. Whenever I tried to have a conversation with her about something deep, she would joke, "Oh, let me put my floods on, it's getting ready to be deep in here!" I always took it to mean that I couldn't be my real and true self with her. So I became something different around her. After time, trying to be someone else wears you out! She made fun of me and therefore I censored myself around her, being careful not to say or do anything that would cause her to want to poke fun at me. Her words changed who I was when I was with her. When I finally got the nerve to speak my peace with her, she did like I was hoping she wouldn't. She judged me and decided that being my friend was too much for her to handle.

All I really wanted from her was her patience and desire to get to know the authentic me. I needed her to be patient because I knew that she would have a difficult time getting to know the real me. The real me is opinionated and passionate about most things. But she never knew that part of me. She only saw the part that I would let her see, because it was easier for her to digest.

We could have had a great relationship had she been able to handle my truth. I didn't need for her to change directly, just be able to handle my truth on a subject when it didn't go parallel to what she thought. I missed her, and wished for something different with her because she was a good person. But I made a promise to myself before my fortieth birthday; that I wouldn't be in a relationship with anyone with whom I couldn't be my true self. Because otherwise I would suffer under the pressure of someone else's idea of "who" I should be.

Women also have bad habits. We can become revenge seekers, jealous and/or bitter. But in contrast, and as I have written, we put others and/or their feelings ahead of our own. We can stifle our own feelings and potential just so that others can feel comfortable in their skin or so others can accept us! That definitely is a bad habit that needs to be put out of its misery.

I wrote earlier about how women give up who they are so that their men can be happy in the life they have with them. But sometimes women do it with other people just so they can get along. Sometimes people can be like a crab in a barrel. One is trying to get out, but the others are trying to pull him back in. Such is life!

I once heard the story of a woman (a single parent) who changed her life by going back to school and continuing her education. She studied for many years to finally get her college degree. Well, all of the people on her job that used to be her friends ostracized her once she got a promotion. They made no apologies for how they treated her because it was obvious to everyone.

Sadly, it seemed as though she cared for what they thought of her. It is sad because she wanted to be friends with the people who tried to make her miserable, even when they showed her they no longer wanted her inside of their circle. Sad also because she couldn't see things as they were: that she should be proud of her accomplishments and not feel guilty for having done something that they were not able to do. Or to allow people such as those to make her feel as though she was missing something by not having them as friends!

Who would want to be friends with someone whose primary intention is to make them feel unwanted? That would be like me losing friends because of my weight loss. Because I am no longer in the same boat, they may sabotage my future weight loss, or decide they no longer have anything in common with me and therefore, choose not to be my friend. But I say another choice would be for those friends to continue to be a part of my life and accept me just as I am because they love me. Or otherwise, for them to man up and decide to use me as an inspiration to change their own lives.

People are always showing us who they are. We just refuse to see it! I am sure that the newly college-educated single mother is proud of her accomplishments. But she has let her desire for approval and friendships overshadow what is more important. She did something that required courage and discipline and she owes it to herself to be proud of what she has done. She shouldn't lessen her accomplishments just so that they will feel comfortable being her friends. If they were her real and true friends, they would have been happy for her. Obviously, the only way for her to regain their friendship is go back to being a crab in that barrel by giving up what she worked so hard for, and belong to their Club of Stupid!

We are all born with different personalities ranging from shy to assertive. Depending on our experiences, certain traits are manifested certain ways when we become adults. I was passive in my former life. That was a very long time ago. I remember when a person would say something cross or hurtful to me, I would just let it slide; I didn't want to hurt their feelings (even when what they said or did hurt me), or I wanted to keep the peace, or I was afraid that maybe they wouldn't like it. Mostly I did it out of fear that they may no longer like me.

I learned that I could be both a likeable person and a person who is not willing to put up with any crap by speaking up for myself. So when someone says or does something to me that in some way attempts to undermine me as a person, I speak up for myself, and I say what needs to be said. Of course, I am not talking about the stranger that took my parking space, even when it was obvious I was waiting for it, because people are crazy! I am talking about the people that I have to live with every day.

We all have probably had fair-weathered relationships. People that only come around, or are only nice to you when they need or want something. You know, like that man that you continue to convince yourself you are only "friends'" with. The one that only calls when he wants a need met, and you oblige him just because you're happy to be in his presence. You're good enough to borrow money from or do the deed with, but you're not good enough to date. We have to learn how to say *NO* to people, especially to the ones who are in our lives because of the season; that is, only for what they can get out of us.

I once met this guy through a friend. I guess she thought he was a good guy, but I thought he was a typical user. Not two weeks after I met him, he was outside of my apartment in his car, with some other friend, waiting for me to come home. I didn't know what the hell he wanted from me. I was a bit nervous because it was past midnight. I barely knew him and he was with other guys I didn't know. I met him one time before this, and I was not at all impressed by our first encounter. I was completely aware of my surroundings and there were some neighbors outside, so I was cool. That night, he asked me if he could borrow some money from me! Who the hell was I to him that he thought it was okay to ask me to do something like that for him without really even knowing him. I told him no. I never saw him again. GOOD!

I would have to assume that he asked because he, just like other men, thought I was desperate for his affections. I was a brand-new and shiny RN. I think he assumed that because I was earning a decent living, I would be only too happy to share it with him!

I learned early on in my adult life that people will walk all over you and use you as a doormat if you let them. And it isn't always from the people temporarily passing through our lives. I have been at some time in my life a doormat for someone to wipe their feet on, and I just laid there; I didn't even rumple with the shifting of the pressure. My experiences have made it unacceptable and inconceivable that I would allow something like that to happen to me now. Because life is learning!

That's another thing women can learn from men. For the most part, men don't let anyone take advantage of them; they easily speak their minds. Many women allow themselves to be taken advantage of all of the time. Men also put themselves first. Depending on the man, they put themselves above everyone else, including their families! It is selfish, because it's all about them. Whether their selfishness is good or bad, it is still something women can learn from.

I grew up poor with a single mother. I can remember looking in the refrigerator and there would only be water, eggs, and cheese.

If we had cereal, we had no milk—if we had milk, we had no cereal. I can remember putting water in my cereal. Dinner could be grits with fried salmon patties (it was actually canned mackerel.) That was some good eating! It wasn't so bad. My mother (with God's help) would somehow always make a way out of no way. On my mother's payday Friday, we would have something special to eat; it gave us something to look forward to.

My children have considerably more than my husband and I had at their age. I have found that we both are guilty of living our lives through our children. We overindulge them with things that we wanted them to have because we didn't have them. Most parents are probably guilty of it. But sometimes, when we do it, it can be at an expense to their potential as productive human beings. Not just because we buy them everything that they want and desire, but also because we don't want to tell them *no*, or be unavailable to them and their wants.

Aside from my mother not being financially sound, she was also not available to chaperone field trips with the school or be a school mom. She was busy working. I can remember wishing that she could be there with me on my field trips, especially when I saw my classmates' mothers with them. I knew that her being there was not an option, and I didn't feel sorry for myself because she wasn't there. She had no time even for herself. Her time was spent either working or taking care of us. When we got old enough to do for ourselves, we did for ourselves. I was able to cook an entire meal by the time I was in middle school. I don't know how suitable for eating it was, but my mother didn't complain. It was one less burden for her to bear.

Seeing my mother struggle taught me how to take care of myself. It took some time, but I have learned how to say *no* to others, including myself. I can easily overextend myself with my time. If the true measure of a good mother is how involved you are in your children's extracurricular activities, then I am a failure.

When I am sent the forms for the PTA from school, I don't even look at them. I will gladly pay any fees, but I don't have the time to participate. I send my children to school to get an education. By the time they get home from school, they need help with their homework, and that's just the beginning. I am not talking about just simple explanations. I am talking about having to explain to them (teach) how to do a lesson from the ground up. When my daughter was in the third grade, because of the requirements for passing to the next grade, it was like she was in college, and I felt like I was in school all over again! (It is my opinion that the schools are so busy trying to maintain their status, that they have made learning no longer fun; rather, too difficult for children.)

I cannot work full time, volunteer *all* of my spare time, be a good mother for my children, and be a whole person to myself simultaneously. I believe a woman can have it "all," just not all at the same time. Thank God that right now, my children are not interested in sports. If they were, I would be in trouble!

It doesn't take much for us women to be made to feel guilty into doing things that we know will be impossible for us to live up to. I am happy to volunteer some of my time, especially for my children's sake, for a project or to help someone, when I can. But women, I say this again, we have to start putting ourselves first so that we can take care of the people who depend on us, including ourselves. As adult women, we have no one to speak up for us, so we MUST speak up for ourselves! So man up and don't be afraid to speak up and stand up for what you should, that is, *you*!

28

For Men Only

It is not my intention for this book to seem as though it is exclusively written for women. Somehow I fear that it will be misunderstood as a book for MB (Male Bashing), but it is not. So for the man who has been brave enough to read my book, this chapter is for you! And the first thing I want you to know is: I am on your side. But I am ultimately on the side of every woman who is struggling in life and in love, because I have been there.

I know many women who believe that their sole and primary function in the relationship is to make you feel like a "man." But whose job is it exactly? Don't misunderstand me. I believe that my job with the man in my life, my husband, is to be his friend, love him (make good love to him) and support him in any way that I can. I also think that my job includes not emasculating him by beating him over the head like a sledgehammer with my words when he doesn't have what I think he should have or do what I want him to. It is my obligation to build him up, because I have his back—but I won't lie to him unnecessarily and I certainly will not uphold him when he has done wrong. I will hold him accountable for the kind of relationship that he wants with me (and his children).

I don't have to see myself naked to know what I am, a woman. I am not confused on the issue. It is not my husband's job to make me feel like a woman. I will admit though, when my husband appreciates my (imperfect) silhouette—it makes me want him more. When he tells me that he loves me (on a regular basis)—I love him more. When he does kind things for me (not for show)—I adore him more. When he takes the time to let me know how great of a mother and wife he thinks I am—I feel appreciated and elevated. When he does everything in his power to please me (because I do everything in my power to be pleasing to him because what we have is reciprocal), I know that I wouldn't want to live my life without him!

Men, you say that you don't want to marry someone who acts like your mother so stop acting like a child! Don't be offended by that statement; listen to what I have to say. Be a grownup by taking responsibility for what is yours: family, children and actions!

This is no time for me to pretend that you have been easy to live or deal with. My husband, early on in the relationship, would accuse me of nagging him when he didn't do what was asked of him. Who did he think he was fooling? Not me. Don't pick a fight with me by trying to turn it around on me and taking the focus off of you! By then, the argument was no longer about what it was supposed to be about: that is, the fact that he was not fulfilling his side of a bargain.

Have you ever worked with someone who spent more time and used up more energy trying to look busy, rather than just doing the damn job? That is what you are doing by not doing your part. But so many people are always trying to not get one-upped or be outdone by anyone. What sense does it make for him to have tried to beat me at a game that was unnecessary to play? And why was he trying to beat me in a game called commitment?

Neither of us had any idea about what it took to be committed to another person inside of a marriage. And what he wanted and expected was different from what I expected or wanted. He wanted to continue to live the life that he had when he was single. He wanted me to be okay with him giving me only a part of him. He wanted his cake and he wanted to be able to eat it when he felt like it! But he couldn't have it all his way. His frustration with me came about because I didn't accept his behavior and he accused me of trying to change him, or make him something that he didn't want to be. And of course, I asked him what was it he wanted to be. Basically he wanted to be left alone. Then, I remarked to him, why be married? He thought he could be married and still live the life of a single man! Men, you can't have it all.

You can't have it all, and we can't do it all! We are not your mothers and we are not your maids. Women may set the tone for the relationship that we have with you, but you are the ones who determine its progression. It takes two to tango. You also know the saying: you catch more bees with honey. If you want more from your woman, do the things that will inspire her to give them to you. As a married woman, nothing turns me on better than when my husband does his part in the life we share. That could be anything from cleaning the kitchen because I cooked the meal to taking out the trash because he sees it needs to be done.

Face it. The woman you marry will change! We all are supposed to change; we become a product of our life experiences. Someone said to me once that his wife was no longer the person he married. He said it as though he was irritated by it (I assume that he was disappointed that she was no longer the same naïve, unaware person that she was when he married her.) But what the real problem was is he didn't change! He wanted what he always had, rather than the possibilities of something better (again, I suppose he just wanted to be left alone like my husband did.)

When we give birth to our children, our bodies change. Unlike the people in Hollywood who have thousands of dollars to spend on personal trainers and customized diet programs, our baby fat doesn't always go away within six weeks of giving birth. When you are not available to do your part with the rearing of your children, she becomes overwhelmed by what needs to be done and no longer has time for you. And it can all spiral out of control: her weight, her sanity, and your needs (if you know what I mean)! Then you become frustrated with her because you think that she only cares for the children's needs. Well, who will, if she doesn't? Another fact that you should know is: children are also what change us. If we don't, they are the ones that suffer the most!

Why are so many of you afraid of commitment? Commitment is not supposed to be the equivalent of walking the plank. It can be an amazing experience when you find the right someone to spend your life with. It is my feeling that when people are not able to commit, it is because they don't know what they want. It is also my feeling that when people don't know what they want, it is because they don't know who they are! So for the many men who are not able to commit, is it because you are still searching for something: the next best thing? Or is it because you don't want to live your life within the boundary of a relationship? As living beings, we all need to have love in our life and a connection to others outside of ourselves. The one-night stands provide a temporary connection to others. In addition, they can offer you the opportunity to find out what you may or may not like about a woman. However, the essential feeling of joy that you get from having someone to share your life with will be lost on someone who is unable to commit. (Nonetheless I understand; you can't miss what you never had!) But don't fear. Give yourself time to find the person meant just for you. You may have to shuck 1,000 oysters to find just one pearl. Just think about it, no commitment!

Can't live with 'em, can't live without 'em. We (women) are

not always easy to live with. I know, ask my husband! But one thing you should know; if you have a woman in your life, she is there because of her choosing! Even if she were a one-night stand, she knew long before you wasted your best lines on her that she was going to bag you! So be careful, if you say or do the wrong thing, it could decrease your chances of getting what you thought was your choice to get!

I could easily say, don't be rude when it comes to not calling the girl as you promised! Believe it or not, I understand. But it is not what you do; it's how you do it. I have found myself in a situation with someone I wanted to be friends with. But after spending a little more time with her, I discovered things about her that I didn't particularly like. It was easier for me to just not call her rather than to tell her how I felt, that is: *you are not my kind of person!* That would have been rude! Frankly, I also feel that it was easier for her as well. It was better that she assumed I was rude than to feel that I had hurt her feelings unnecessarily. She is not a bad person, just not someone that I can be a friend with. What was important to her was not what is important to me. Our lifestyles are so completely different.

It would be easy for us to label you as the villain when you don't call as you said you would. I think that most women would just be satisfied that you no longer straddle the fence. Choose a side; call her or don't. If you call her, call her with the intention of getting to know her. And if it is not working out as you expected, say so. A real woman can handle the truth! If you don't call her, fine. But don't get started with something that you know you have no intentions of finishing. And don't lie to her just so that you can buy yourself some time; that is rude!

Why do you lie? Lying to me is, for the most part, an unnecessary evil. The intention with lying is to create a false sense of reality. There cannot be true happiness in a relationship when it is based on lies. Sometimes you lie just to be able to close the deal. But even after the deal has been closed, the truth comes out! And instead of looking like a champion, you look like a loser because you are found out as a fraud! It just *don't* look good! By lying you're telling people that you are unsatisfied with the life you are living and therefore pretending to be someone you aren't. So who wants to be with someone that even you don't want to be?

Believe it or not, most of the women that I know aren't looking for a "rich" man. They are just looking for someone decent to share their lives with. (I personally would live in a shack with my husband as long as our family is intact.) They want someone they can depend on, someone who will have their back, and someone who can change a light bulb.

Speaking of changing light bulbs, it's a good segue into what I want to speak about. It is shocking that we have so many men who are unable to change a damn flat tire! The flat tire is an analogy for the many things that men used to "bring to the table" in a relationship. My mother is from the old school. I remember vividly her saying that she would never date a man unless he could provide for her in some way. For her that meant paying her bills. Now I don't think that a man should necessarily be responsible for his woman's bills (unless of course money is of no issue), but I do believe that he should be "putting out" by doing his part. I have friends in relationships with men who don't know how to change the locks on the door, how to change a flat tire or fix what's ailing a car! What the fuck is that? You tell me! And as a matter of fact, as a woman, my man had better be able to either fix sumthin' or be able to pay for it to get fixed!

Have an open mind. Some of us have natural talents and some things come easy. Being a good kisser came natural for me. My sexual competence, early on, needed some improvement, but I was a quick study. If your woman suggests that the two of you try something different, don't assume that she has done "it" with some other man! And don't assume that she is telling you that you suck. (And what if you sucked? Wouldn't you like to be sexually pleasing to her? Would you be comfortable with the thought that you probably weren't the *best* lover that she's ever had?) Don't take it as an attack on your ego. It would make no sense for your woman to be unsatisfied in bed just because you can't handle the truth. Why should she have to suffer? And if the both of you don't know how to approach the subject, my suggestion is that you both sit on the bed (butt ass naked) facing each other (talking and touching) while asking the other what is pleasing to them. And don't forget to keep the lights on!

Just so that you know, if a woman sleeps with you only after knowing you for a short time, it doesn't make her easy. It just means that she lives in the year 2011. We don't live in a time where we have to wait on you for everything! We can do more. We can have more. But the one thing we can't have is; *everything*! She still needs you. No matter how accomplished she may be; she still desires someone to share her life with. But if you don't do right, she will resign herself to a life without you; then where will we be?

I know it's hard out there for a P-I-M-P! You have gotten a raw deal. You have been raised to believe that you are something special (and you are) just because you were born with a penis. You have received special treatment all of your lives because you were born with that penis. You were brought into a world with many expectations for your life, but never being made fully aware of how to achieve those expectations. I can only imagine that it would be overwhelming not to have a sense of myself outside of the one thing that makes you what you are: a penis! As a woman, the one thing I am sure of is that you are more than your penis; you are what we need. You are what we want and desire. You, along with us, are necessary for making this world go around!

As I have said, men can have a lot of bad habits. And with your bad habits, there are also some good ones of you out there. I know because I am married to one. He isn't perfect, (and neither am I) but I think I'll keep him! It's a jungle out there!

What Do You Want?

29

What do you want? That's probably a harder question to answer than who are you? The hardest thing in life is to know what it is that you want. Once you know what you want, the rest is easy. Making it happen may not seem easy, especially if its accomplishment involves something that is maybe out of reach, such as money, time, connections, etc. But it sure is a hell of a lot easier knowing what it is that you want than not knowing. Knowing is like having half of the battle won. It's like going through life not knowing what you're doing or what to expect. Or like going through a fog not knowing what you're looking for and there is no end in sight.

When I was in college, there were a lot of students who were unsure of what their major would be. For a couple of years they would just take the basic college courses until they could figure it out! That seemed simple enough, but life is a little more complicated than that.

Don't go through life not knowing what it is that you want from it. If you don't know, take the time to be quiet with yourself to figure it out. Let the decision of what you want be authentically yours, and no one else's. Don't allow yourself to be pressured into doing anything because you think it is what someone else wants.

As you already know, my husband was married to another woman before he married me. According to him, he knew that it was a mistake to marry her when she was walking down the aisle. He says he did it because he thought he was doing the right thing; she was supposedly pregnant. I could say that it was admirable of him to want to marry her so that he could be a good father for his potential child. Shortly after they married, she announced, after he came home from work, that she had a miscarriage! He never saw the doctor or any paperwork stating that information. I told him so, and I am telling you, that it was STUPID!

It was stupid because he made a decision to marry her knowing full well that it wasn't what he wanted. It seems obvious that it was what she wanted. I am not sure, but it sounded to me like she was attempting to trap him in a relationship that she must have known he was otherwise not interested in having, contrary to her. Does that mean that he should have had to suffer in a relationship with a woman because she was the mother of his child? I say no. Not only would he be unhappy, so would she. In addition, the child would have been brought up in a loveless home. He should have just taken some time to let the information marinate so he could sort through his feelings. The time taken would have been crucial to making the right decision for all involved. But what am I saying...he is married to me now!

Qualify it! Whatever it is that you want, define it. If it's happiness, be your own source of happiness by living the life of knowing what you want from it. If it is the companionship of a man, know what it is that you want and expect of him. If it is a good life, know what that means to you!

30

Bee Happy

Happiness. What will be required in order for you to be happy in the life that you are living? Whatever you think the ingredient may be, I can tell you that the only thing needed is your desire for it. I go to a job where, on many days, someone has commented to me—"Why are you always so happy?" or "Why are you so *damn* happy?" As though it's some kind of disease they don't want to catch! My reply is plainly, "Because I woke up this morning!" I titled this chapter "Bee Happy" for the purpose of emphasizing the word "Be." "Being" is an action, and it enlists you to do something about "something." The purpose is to stress to you that the only thing you need to do in order to "bee" happy is to just do it!

Most people are unhappy because they go through life not being aware of their place in the world or their potential impact on it. Outside of my being healthy, as well as my children and family being healthy, or besides something that would involve compromising my principles, generally speaking, there is nothing that could make me feel down for longer than it would take to just shake it off. People spend way too much time and use so much energy complaining about nothing. Time that could be better spent trying to get whatever it is that could make them happy, and make them better people for themselves and their family.

Even when my husband and I argue with one another, it has no impact on my happiness. He used to get so angry with me when we argue and I go on with life as though the fight never happened. Hell, I can remember early in the marriage he would ask me after an argument, "You want a divorce?" It was amusing to me that he couldn't separate my being disappointed in him and still be able to love him at the same time.

Over time he has been able to understand the difference, but now he doesn't understand how we can argue and I can still be happy. My happiness belongs to me and no one else. No one else but I am in control of it or have the power to manipulate it. I have said to him, "Believe it or not, my happiness is not dependent on whether you are happy, or whether you are happy in your life with me. My happiness exists outside of you and has nothing to do with you!"

Have you ever driven somewhere and you didn't remember how you got there? You didn't remember seeing any of the landmarks you passed, the people walking by, or how beautiful the sky was. Many of us are guilty of it; daydreaming while driving. The difference is that some of us go through life daydreaming, being disconnected to the world outside of us.

Who could not see the blessing of being able to wake up to another day, *every day*? To not be able to see God's glory wherever you turn: When you look at your children, to be able to go to a job that you complain about, or to actually have a job. When it's raining outside to serve its purpose—to make the flowers bloom. To be able to see a sunset, to watch your children laugh and play and be happy—to be able to cry, to smile, to see, to taste, to feel, to hear, and to smell. Nothing in life is guaranteed; nothing lasts forever. At any moment it could be taken away, so be ever *GRATEFUL!*

Don't go through life daydreaming. Be aware of your surroundings, your place in them, and how you have the power to change them. Have a connection with yourself and the people around you, even the ones that you don't know. I have walked an entire corridor while someone was walking toward me going in the opposite direction. The reaction can be a simple hello, a smile, or the extreme; killing themselves by turning their heads around 180 degrees, just to keep from acknowledging another soul's presence!

There are people who have worse circumstances than others, yet they find a way to be happy with what they have. If we are not happy, it is because we want something that we don't have or something is not meant for us. It may be because we don't know what we want or how to get what we want. It could be because we are waiting for someone else to give us what we need and want.

Remember: being alive means that a person has survived something. Hard times and heartbreak are nothing that is exclusive to one person. We have to learn how to be grateful for *EVERYTHING*, including our past disappointments and failures, because without them we have no basis for growth and therefore, true happiness.

Many people complain about their circumstances even when their circumstances aren't so bad. No matter how terrible you think you got it, someone has it worse (or vice versa). It could take a catastrophic illness or incident to make those same people realize that they spent too much time complaining about something trivial.

Even when we aren't aware of it, we all take things for granted. I know my husband thinks I take him for granted. He thinks that all I do is complain about what he doesn't do, rather than pay attention to what he does. But what I know for sure is that he has done nothing but take me for granted since we've been married. He says that I should be grateful to have a husband who doesn't cheat on me, hang out with his friends every night or when he goes, stay out all night long. My feeling in the matter is; IT IS WHAT HE IS SUPPOSED TO DO! He gets no special treatment for doing his part, as he should. Hell, if he mops the floor, he expects a rub on the top of his head, and the trumpets to sound. I did housework regularly without any expectation for him to notice. I remember cleaning the windowsills and he said, "Wow, look at all that dirt; I didn't know they needed to be cleaned," as if all this time they cleaned themselves.

If I take my husband for granted, it is only because he doesn't always give me what I need. That is why my happiness cannot depend on whether or not he is happy in his life with me. I love him dearly and deeply, but I will never let him think that it is okay for him to only think about what it is that *he* needs from our relationship.

When I was at my heaviest, my husband was less attracted to me. I know because he has said so. I always felt his love, but I could tell, even without him saying so, that he didn't like the way I looked. He even asked me once, "Why can't you just lose the weight for me?"

I could try and pretend that his words weren't hurtful, but they were. They even pissed me off. But whatever his words were, they were also honest. I tried hard not to notice, in the mirror, what everyone noticed when they saw me: that I was not living the life that I intended for myself. But, my weight problem had nothing to do with him. If I had made it about him and what he wanted, I would have not been as successful at it. I could only lose it when I was ready.

I am grateful that he is a man who loved me regardless of my weight (big girls need love, too), although he had every reason to feel the way he felt. His love for me was more important to him than what I looked like at the time. And because he hung in there with me, he now has (what most men would consider having their cake and eating it, too) sex with another woman, me!

Giving in to what he wants from me instead of what I want for myself would change who I am. Not being me is the same as being someone else. Being someone else means living a life that is not my own. I don't want to forget that I have a purpose in life and give up opportunities for my happiness. Not being happy means becoming indifferent. I don't want to become numb to my surroundings and unimpressed by greatness wherever I see it... in me!

Change Your Life

31

I am not a prisoner of my past. I am a product of it. Whether my experiences were good or bad, they were mine. I own them. I am not ashamed of them. I revel in them. My experiences deeply changed who I am.

I want to tell you a story about how I learned to read. When I was in the first grade, I didn't know how to read. We, the kids, were formed in a circle. We each had to read a passage (the same passage) from a book. The teacher wanted to start with me but I didn't want to be the one to start. So I asked to go last. (The teacher, I am sure, took notice of my lack of confidence, and therefore allowed me to be the last to read.)

I watched every word as it was being read and memorized each one. By the time it was my turn to read, I was ready! I stumbled with a few of the words, but got encouragement from the teacher and the other students. I felt good. I felt confident!

At the age of seven, that experience put me on the road to become a fast learner. It taught me to pay attention. I didn't like not knowing how to do something that others did easily. I also didn't want to be teased for not being able to do something they could. Or because it was something they thought I should be able to do. I wanted to be just like them. I wanted to fit in. As adults, I notice that many people pretend to be something they are not. I would assume it is so they can fit in.

I am not ashamed of my past because it helped to define the person I am today. When we allow our past to put us in the position to cower, we give in to it, either because we are ashamed of it or because we don't want to be judged. That's when the pretending starts. When you speak your truth out loud, you will find that others have the same in common with you. Therefore, we can all fit in, if we were just willing to be open with ourselves first, and then with others.

In order to change your life, you have to be ready, willing and able. Because some people have limitations, they may not be able. Because some people don't want to dig deep, they may not be ready. And because some people don't want to acknowledge that there needs to be a change, they may not be willing. But whatever your individual circumstances are, after the acknowledgment of there needing to be a change in your life, you have to have all of the ingredients to achieve it. Not one, not two, but all three. It will require the readiness in your determination, the willingness of your persistence, and your ability to be dedicated despite your many obstacles to a new you.

Only you know if you got what you needed growing up. It's so easy to blame our parents or our past for everything that is wrong with our life now. But let me tell you, you've got to stop blaming the things of the past for the life you have now. Don't let your past harden your heart. No matter how bad it was—its purpose was only for you to learn from. You, as an adult, are to blame for the life you have now. If you continue to blame your past experiences for your present and your future, you will *NEVER* have the life that you are meant to lead. I recognize that some people's past experiences have had a very disturbing impact on their future—circumstances the knowledge of which, I am sure, would make most of us tremble. But because I am an optimist, I believe that no matter how difficult a past experience was; we all have the ability to get past it, either with supportive family, friends or with some therapy.

I have many challenges, and right now raising our children, our daughter especially, is a major challenge. *EVERY DAY* her father and I have to remind her of what it is she has to do around the house! I had a conversation with her late one night because yet again she had to be reminded of her duties. I told her that the fact that she has to perform her assigned chores is not because I didn't want to do it, but because she has to learn responsibility. She has consistently failed to perform a task without her father or me reminding her to do so constantly. I told her the point of doing her chores is to teach her how to use her brain; to think, become disciplined, have accountability and not be lazy. She looked at me stunned, because I believe she thought we told her to do it because *WE* didn't want to do it!

I was starting to notice that it didn't matter what her father and I wanted her to do, she'd still do what *she* wanted to do, but we are not having that! I explained to her: from the time that she wakes up in the morning, she needs to start focusing on her days' plan and try and keep herself on track. I know she will need to be reminded from time to time, but I'm hopeful that with time, she will start to want to do differently, not for us, but for herself.

I tell her frequently that she can be anything that she wants to be. I tell her that I want her to do better in school, not just to get good grades, but because I want her to care about her grades. I tell her I want her to take care of her things, not because I don't want anything broken, but because I want to know that she is respectful of the things that her father and I work hard for her to have. I can want all day long for a good life for her, but ultimately she has to want it for herself!

It has always been my intention to start early with teaching my children life lessons. Sow the seeds of self-love, self-respect, and self-confidence within them. Above all else, I want my children to be happy! I want them to be able to grow up in a world and be okay with who they are. Because I know, they have yet to learn, that they live in a world where people will judge them wrongly just because of the color of their skin.

I want them to be able to walk into a room, and without them having to utter a word, all can see there is something special about them. I want them to believe in themselves, think for themselves and be able to stand in a room full of people who don't necessarily share their view, and I want them to be able to stand for what they believe in.

I don't know how they will turn out as time goes on, but I am doing my part. I pray every day for them, and for myself, so that I can be the mother that they need me to be, because it is not easy! Life will be hard enough for them. Not having a good foundation can be a formula for disaster. But I am a firm believer; it is not what happens to us that determines who we become, but what we allow ourselves to become.

Getting back to you... What kind of woman are you? Are you nurturing, compassionate and loving not just to others but also to yourself? Are you gossipy, mean, angry or jealous-hearted? Are you the kind of woman who will tolerate any kind of behavior from the people in your life because you think you have no choice? Remember, you always have a choice!

It takes an awful lot of courage to change your life. Because when you change, you expose yourself to personal criticism and judgment, and it is not easy. Not only that, but you expose yourself to criticism and judgment from people outside of yourself. My oldest sister divorced a man that she had been with for more than twenty-five years. She can't explain it to herself why she stayed so long. Ultimately, I think it is because she became accustomed to being in a relationship that was suicidal to her spirit. She started to think it was all she was capable of having or deserved. Fortunately, someone finally got through to her...*SHE* finally realized a life far greater than the one she had been living for all of those years!

Our experiences are what make us who we are, especially the bad stuff. If everything in your life were rosy, then you'd have nothing to compare it to, to know how good *it* really is. Every bad experience happens for us to learn from it. The problem is that many of us try to change the experience (or the person), and then it is no longer a life lesson; it becomes something less than authentic. It becomes artificial.

In the beginning of the book I started off by saying how my husband said that I saved his life. I say that he saved his own life! The only thing I did was influence the change that he made in himself. He had to want it for himself. All I did was provide an avenue for him to change by not making excuses for his behavior or treating him like a child. I held him accountable for the kind of relationship that *he* wanted with me, because I knew what I expected and needed from him. If we had not survived, it would have been because he decided that he didn't want to be a better man, and he knew that I would have never sacrificed myself for him.

From the start I also wrote about the different things that influence the journey of relationships—commitment, infidelity, accountability, trust and honesty, communication, and real love, among other things. These are just words, but are given life during the evolution of the relationship. How they manifest themselves in the relationship is dependent upon how you understand what they have to do with you.

You have to be committed to yourself, make a pledge to never give up on yourself or what you want for yourself. Have fidelity and be faithful to yourself so that you can stick to your commitments. Be accountable to realize that ultimately it is your life, and only you are to blame for not living the life of your intention. Trust yourself and be honest—because you have to be honest about the life you want and the life you live to be able to trust yourself. Communicate with yourself. Intuition is a God-given gift. If you feel something is amiss, trust yourself to allow your inner voice to speak. And love yourself, because no one can love what you don't. Most importantly, no one can love you better than you!

Just like the job you go to every day to earn a paycheck, you have to put the same amount of effort, if not more, into becoming the person that you want to be. If you are not living the life that you deserve, don't be pissed off at the world because you think it owes you something, and this is because *you* owe *yourself* everything.

Life is too short—this is not a dress rehearsal, this is *your* life! You only live it once; there is no "Take 2!" My sister passed away in a terrible apartment fire; she was only forty-five years old. It's over for her. If there was anything that she wanted to accomplish, she can't anymore.

After she passed away, I saw many things in perspective and I was determined to make some changes, to honor her memory, but also to honor myself first and foremost. For example, I had gone my entire adult life not knowing how to swim and being very afraid to get in the water. I would hyperventilate when I entered the pool with the water at chest level. When she died, I made a commitment to myself to learn how to swim, or to at least be comfortable in water without freaking out.

I took a swimming class along with my younger sister. Many times I would look at the door, while in the water, and think to myself, "I can just leave and never come back and no one would care!" But I realized *I* would have cared. I would know that I didn't finish something that I started. My sister was my inspiration to do something that I always wanted to do, because she couldn't ever again.

Hopefully, you are not feeling sorry for yourself, asking, "Why me?" I remember something vital that my mother said to me once when I got some bad news: "Why not you?" Then she went on to say to me, "If *it* happened to someone else, you wouldn't have given it any thought, but it's happened to you, so what are you going to do about it?" I was dumbfounded because I thought that she was supposed to feel pity for me and thus make things better. But she had no time for that; her intention was for me to get up off my ass, and change my position in the matter. SO WHAT ARE *YOU* GOING TO DO?

About the Author

C T Shackleford was born, raised and earned her college degree in Mobile, Alabama.

Shortly after marriage, she relocated to the suburbs of Atlanta, GA where she is now raising her two school-aged children alongside her husband (the oldest a daughter, and a son). C T continues to work as an RN for Cardiac Services at a major hospital in the Atlanta area.

For more information, please visit www.ctscorner.com.